Writing Program Administration

MW00513442

Journal of the
Council of Writing Program Administrators

Editors
Barbara L'Eplattenier .... University of Arkansas at Little Rock
Lisa Mastrangelo ....Centenary University of New Jersey

Assistant Editors
Sarah Ricard .... University of Arkansas at Little Rock

Book Review Editor
Norbert Elliot...University of South Florida

Associate Book Review Editor
Jacob Babb.. Indiana University Southeast

Ads Manager
Kelsie Walker .... Ball State University

Editorial Board
Bradley Bleck .... Spokane Falls Community College
Micheal Callaway... Mesa Community College
Norbert Elliot...University of South Florida
Casie Fedukovich .... North Carolina State University
Tarez Samra Graban.. Florida State University
Kristine Hansen .... Brigham Young University
Al Harahap .... University of Arizona, WPA-GO Representative
Asao B. Inoue...................................... University of Washington, Tacoma
Seth Kahn..West Chester University
Carrie Leverenz ....Texas Christian University
Paul Kei Matsuda ....Arizona State University
Mark McBeth........................John Jay College of Criminal Justice/CUNY
Laura Micciche..University of Cincinnati
Charles Paine .... University of New Mexico
E. Shelley Reid .... George Mason University
Rochelle (Shelley) Rodrigo..................................Old Dominion University
Ellen Schendel.. Grand Valley State University
Wendy Sharer...East Carolina University
Amy Ferdinandt Stolley ....Saint Xavier University
Martha A. Townsend... University of Missouri
Elizabeth Vander Lei .... Calvin College
Scott Warnock... Drexel University

WPA: Writing Program Administration is published twice per year—fall and spring—
by the Council of Writing Program Administrators. Production and printing of
WPA: Writing Program Administration is managed by Parlor Press.

Council of Writing Program Administrators

Authors' Guide

WPA: Writing Program Administration publishes empirical and theoretical research on issues in writing program administration. We publish a wide range of research in various formats, research that not only helps both titled and untitled administrators of writing programs do their jobs, but also helps our discipline advance academically, institutionally, and nationally. *WPA: Writing Program Administration* is published twice per year: fall and spring. Possible topics of interest include:

- writing faculty professional development
- writing program creation and design
- critical analysis and applications of discipline or national policies and statements that impact writing programs
- labor conditions: material, practical, fiscal
- WAC/WID/WC/CAC (or other sites of communication/writing in academic settings)
- teaching multimodal writing
- teaching in digital spaces
- theory, practice, and philosophy of writing program administration
- outreach and advocacy
- writing program assessment
- WPA history and historical work
- national and regional trends in education and their impact on WPA work
- issues of professional advancement and writing program administration
- diversity and WPA work
- writing programs in a variety of educational locations (SLAC, HBCU, two-year colleges, Hispanic schools, non-traditional schools, concurrent work)
- interdisciplinary work that informs WPA practices

This list is not comprehensive. If you have questions about potential work for *WPA: Writing Program Administration*, please query the editors. We are particularly interested in publishing new voices and new topics.

Submission Guidelines

Check the website for complete submissions guidelines. Please include the cover sheet available at http://wpacouncil.org/info-for-authors. In general submissions should:

- be between 3,000–7,000 words; longer and shorter pieces will rarely be considered
- follow *MLA Style Manual and Guide to Scholarly Publishing* (most current edition)

- have identifying information removed for peer review: author name(s), track changes, comments, and properties cleared throughout
- include a short running head with page numbers
- include an abstract (200 words max) as part of the manuscript, following the title and preceding the body of the text
- have an accurate and correctly formatted works cited page
- include the cover sheet
- be saved as a .doc, .docx, or .rtf file. Do not send .pdf files. If you have special formatting needs, contact the editors.

More information regarding the formatting of the manuscript (specifically endnotes, tables, and pictures) is available at http://wpacouncil.org/node/1812. Manuscripts that don't conform to the requirements will be returned to the author with a request to reformat.

Reviews

WPA: Writing Program Administration publishes review essays of books related to writing programs and their administration. Publishers are invited to recommend appropriate books to bookreviews@wpacouncil.org. If you are interested in reviewing texts, please contact the book review editor at bookreviews@wpacouncil.org

Announcements and Calls

Relevant announcements and calls for papers and/or conference participation will be published as space permits. Announcements should not exceed 500 words, and calls for proposals/participation should not exceed 1,000 words. Please include contact information and links for further information. Submission deadlines in calls should be no earlier than January 1 for the fall/winter issue and June 1 for the spring issue. Please email your calls and announcements to journal@wpacouncil.org and include the text both in the body of the message and as an MS Word or RTF attachment.

Correspondence

Correspondence relating to the journal, submissions, or editorial issues should be sent to journal@wpacouncil.org

Subscriptions

WPA: Writing Program Administration is published twice per year—fall and spring by the Council of Writing Program Administrators. Members of the Council of Writing Program Administrators receive a subscription to the journal as part of their membership. Join at http://wpacouncil.org/join-renew. Active members have access to online versions of current and past issues through the WPA website http:wpacouncil.org/journalarchives. Library subscription information is available at http://wpacouncil.org/library-memberships.

Writing Program Administration

Journal of the
Council of Writing Program Administrators
Volume 40.3 (Summer 2017)

Special Issue: Ability and Accessibility

Contents

Letter from the Editor 7
    Kathleen M. Hunzer

Ma(r)king a Difference: Challenging Ableist Assumptions in Writing
Program Policies 10
    Melissa Nicolas

Toward Inclusive and Multi-Method Writing Assessment for College
Students with Learning Disabilities: The (Universal) Story of Max 23
    Steven J. Corbett

Failures to Accommodate: GTA Preparation as a Site for a
Transformative Culture of Access 39
    Casie J. Fedukovich and Tracy Ann Morse

Saying No to the Checklist: Shifting from an Ideology of Normalcy
    to an Ideology of Inclusion in Online Writing Instruction 61
    Sushil K. Oswal and Lisa Meloncon

Kindness in the Writing Classroom: Accommodations for
    All Students 78
    Kelly A. Shea

Reviews

Developing Inclusive and Accessible Online Writing Instruction:
    Supporting OWI Principle 1 94
    Brenta Blevins

Rereading and Retelling Rhetoric's Embodied Stories   100
Ella R. Browning

Toward an Interpretive Framework for Access in Writing Programs   105
Annika Konrad

Centering Madness in the Academe: Supporting and Learning from Mental Disability   111
Elisabeth L. Miller

Making Space to Engage Difference in the Classroom   117
Kelly A. Whitney

Letter from the Editor

Kathleen M. Hunzer

In November of 2011, when Temple Grandin spoke on our campus, she shared that when she thinks about ideas and concepts, she thinks not in words but in pictures. She also spoke about how rather than thinking in a top down fashion, she thinks in a bottom up style, which makes traditional writing tasks difficult for her. The example she cited was this: think about the word *dog*. When a person who is not on the autism spectrum (sometimes this person is called neurotypical) hears the word *dog*, that person can generalize about the term *dog*. When someone on the spectrum who is a primarily visual learner hears the word *dog*, however, very specific images come to mind rather than a generalized notion: a poodle from a neighboring house, a Doberman seen at the park last week, a pug from a TV commercial, a German Shepard that patrolled the airport last month, etc. In other words, this person sees each of these as distinct pictures that flash through her mind as she thinks of the word *dog* rather than a generalized image of a *dog*. In order to then generalize, the person with autism who is primarily a visual learner looks for the elements that tie all dogs together: They are all classified as canine, all have the same shaped nose, all have the same basic physiology, etc.

As I drove home that night after her talk, I had an odd thought: here is Temple Grandin—a highly intelligent, internationally-known, and well-published person who has practically single-handedly improved her industry, yet if she were in *a traditional* composition class, she likely would have done poorly because her thought processes do not match the neurotypical policies and assignments used in many traditional writing classes. As I imagined this brilliant mind not doing well in one of my first-year writing classes, my brain buzzed with questions: how would other people who think like this survive a college writing class that privileges linear top down thinking? How does someone who thinks in images translate that to the standard form of the essay? Does the dominant paradigm used in most

WPA: Writing Program Administration, vol. 40, no. 3, 2017, pp. 7–9.

7

writing classes accommodate or alienate someone like Temple? Would Temple have failed simply because of a neurotypical bias?

At this same time, I was the Director of Written Communication for our two- or three-course composition sequence (depending on placement scores) that served approximately 1,500 in-coming students each year. In typical WPA fashion, I was the point person for all instructors of these writing classes, which included both tenure-line and adjunct instructors, and as the only person formally trained in Composition and Rhetoric in the department, I quickly learned that I was expected to be the answer person and the problem-solver for all things related to our writing sequence. In hallway or drop-in meetings with the writing instructors, I answered a plethora of questions, but as I thought more about what Temple said, my brain honed in on some of the most recent questions raised by our instructors: Why am I responsible for accommodating students with disabilities? Why is asking a student to be a note-taker my job? What do I do with a student with Tourette's who shouts out in class? If students can't control their anxiety, should they even be in college? How do I get the kid in the back of the room to stop rocking back and forth and tracing the map of Egypt as I lecture? Some instructors asking the questions seemed annoyed that they had to find ways to accommodate all students, but more of the instructors were sincerely interested in providing a classroom experience that would help all students succeed.

In true serendipitous fashion, after hearing Temple speak and completing a sabbatical exploring the connections of Ability Studies and Composition, I was asked to be the inaugural chair of the CWPA Disabilities Committee, and in our first year, we created our Position Statement on Accessibility. We disseminated this statement at the Savannah, Georgia meeting of the CWPA. The audience was very interested in what we wrote, offered helpful feedback, and agreed that we all should commit to being more award of issues of ability and accessibility as they pertain to our roles as WPAs. By the end of the conference, we were all committed to raising awareness of these issues, which included future CWPA conferences having an Ability and Accessibility Information table as well as more presentations about these issues. Happily, from this experience came the invitation to compile this special issue of our journal, which is what you will read today. Only being able to select a few articles to include was difficult since there are a multitude of perspectives to explore when addressing issues of ability and accessibility in our programs, so I selected pieces that discuss some key aspects of our jobs.

First, Melissa Nicolas invites us to think holistically about these issues by examining if some of our program policies are problematic in her article "Ma(r)king a Difference: Challenging Ablest Assumptions in Writing Program Policies." Following this, Steven J. Corbett explores the issue of assessment in his piece "Toward Inclusive and Multi-Modal Writing Assessment for College Students with Learning Disabilities: The (Universal) Story of Max." Casie Fedukovich and Tracy Morse then address an issue pertinent to many WPAs jobs—GTA preparation—in their piece "Failures to Accommodate: GTA Preparation as a Site for a Transformative Culture of Access." Because online writing classes and teacher preparation are a concern of WPAs, Sushil K. Oswal and Lisa Meloncon's piece "Saying No to the Checklist: Shifting From an Ideology of Normalcy to an Ideology of Inclusion in Online Writing Instruction" raises key issues about online writing design. The final essay, Kelly A. Shea's "Kindness in the Writing Classroom: 'Accommodations' for All Students," asks us to step back and consider that some of the accommodations we enact for people with ability and accessibility challenges may be beneficial to all students. "As a whole, I believe this issue—along with perceptive reviews by Brenta Blevins , Ella R. Browning, Annika Konrad, Elisabeth L. Miller, and Kelly A. Whitney— will open our minds to new ideas, challenge us to re-think some of our practices and pedagogies, and will, most importantly, get our community talking so that we can all serve our students in the best way possible. Enjoy!

Kathleen Hunzer is the Director of the Chancellor's Scholars, Honors Program, and Falcon Scholars and is a professor of English at the University of Wisconsin-River Falls, a four-year comprehensive public university. She is the author of journal articles as well as scholarly presentations and published the edited collection Collaborative Learning and Writing: Essays on Using Small Groups in Teaching English and Composition. *She has taught a variety of writing theory and practice classes as well as disabilities studies. Her first young adult novel,* Always a Reason to Smile, *encourages readers to embrace all friendships regardless of ability status.*

Ma(r)king a Difference: Challenging Ableist Assumptions in Writing Program Policies

Melissa Nicolas

Abstract

WPAs are tasked with creating and maintaining writing programs' policies and procedures; however, we have paid surprisingly little critical attention to how our program policies function as rhetorical constructs, particularly in terms of disability. Using the commonplace of the mandatory attendance policy, I explore ways that ableism—the privileging of a hypothetical "perfect" body— permeates some of our most basic practices. In this essay, I argue that even in cases where we decide to make exceptions to our mandatory attendance policy, we do nothing to address the fundamental problem with the policy itself: its failure to take into account the embodied, material realties of our students' lives. Indeed, I demonstrate that the mandatory attendance policy creates the very conditions under which we need to make multiple exemptions, creating disabling situations for our students and our instructors. I conclude by calling for an application of the principles of UDL in policy-making.

Introduction

It is week ten of a sixteen-week semester. Three different FYW instructors have scheduled appointments with me (the WPA) to talk about students who have accrued enough absences that their grades should be penalized according to our writing program attendance policy, which allows students to miss a week's worth of classes after which their course grades are penalized (Appendix A). The instructors want to discuss their students with me because something doesn't feel right about penalizing them. Here are the students' stories:[1]

> Leandra has told her FYW instructor that she hasn't been sleeping or eating well for the past two weeks. Up until week seven, she hadn't

WPA: Writing Program Administration, vol. 40, no. 3, 2017, pp. 10–22.

10

missed any classes, was an active class participant, and was turning in exemplary work, but over the course of the past few weeks, she has been silent in class, has missed a few minor assignments, and has been absent four times.

Tighe sometimes uses a wheelchair and other times uses crutches to navigate campus. He turns in assignments on time and his papers have all earned passing grades. His class participation is solid. However, because he is often not present by the time his instructor takes roll, Tighe is usually marked "tardy" according to the writing program policy, so by this point in the semester, he has accumulated enough absences (three tardies = one absence) that his course grade is now being affected.[2]

Jasmine is struggling in her writing class. She received a D on her first formal paper and is holding a C- average in the course. Her attendance is spotty at best, and she often falls asleep in class. She has not responded to her instructor's emails about her course grade being affected by her multiple absences.

I doubt any of these scenarios are unfamiliar to WPAs or experienced teachers. Semester after semester, I have conversations about why instructors might want to relax the attendance policy. Instructors who seek me out about situations like the ones I just described say something feels "off" about enforcing the attendance policy. What these instructors are sensing is the fact that our attendance policy is not predicated on the reality of an embodied student; therefore, when students do not perform/present in certain predetermined ways, ways outlined in our attendance policy, there is confusion about how to treat them. We—Leandra's, Tighe's, and Jasmine's teachers and WPA—do not know for sure what is causing their absences; we can and will ask them, but as Jasmine has made clear, some students are just not interested in sharing—or cannot—talk to us. But even if we decide to suspend the attendance policy in these cases, we will have done nothing to address the fundamental problem with the mandatory attendance policy: It fails to take into account the embodied, material realties of our students' lives.

Mandatory attendance policies (and some other writing program policies), as I will demonstrate in this essay, are premised on ableist assumptions of a "normal" student body. These assumptions actually undermine writing programs' attempts to promote equity, diversity, and social justice by reifying normate behaviors. While the spirit of mandatory attendance policies is laudable and keenly in line with some of composition studies' core beliefs—particularly, that community is essential for becoming a better writer so students need to show up and participate in such a community if they are to get anything out of our classes (also see Prendergast)—the purpose of this article is to challenge WPAs to begin taking a more critical look at what our policies actually force us to practice. By challenging some of our commonplace policies such as mandatory attendance, I hope to provide WPAs with a generative space from which to start rethinking and remodeling not just our classrooms but also the programs that feed, nurture, and support those classrooms.

Biomedical and Social Models of Disability

Western higher education is grounded in a Platonic version of an idealized student body.[3] This body is young, healthy, white, male, and usually straight (Davis 3). This body can sit for anywhere from 50 minutes to 3 hours and listen to a lecture and take perfect notes by hand, aided by a photographic memory. This body is not shy, never experiences anxiety or mental illness, can control all of its bodily functions, has 20/20 vision, excellent hearing, and perfect gross and fine motor skills. Its limbs can easily navigate a campus of any size, moving with speed and ease between buildings in short amounts of time. This body can also read, write, and speak without effort and can process information in a linear fashion; it is just as fluent with text as with speech as with manipulating objects, and it has total and precise recall abilities (Dolmage, "Writing" 110–115). A common term for this mythical body is "normate."

As disability scholars have reminded us, the normate body does not actually exist, but rather, it becomes an impossible standard that we all fail to meet (Davis). The above description of the normate student body is not written anywhere, but the assumption of it is hiding in plain sight in many of our policies.[4] Dolmage and Lewiecki-Wilson tell us, "The normate position occupies a supposedly preordained, unproblematic, transparent, and unexamined centrality. A normate culture, then, continuously reinscribes the centrality, naturality, neutrality, and unquestionability of this normate position" (24).

As WPAs, we have an obligation to our students and our writing programs to start chipping away at these embedded assumptions. As Jay Dolmage suggests:

> If the composition teacher wants to treat students ethically and respectfully, she must consider the spaces where she teaches in terms of disciplinary attitudes, but also in terms of bricks and mortar, walls and steps that exclude bodies. The disciplinary and the institutional, the discursive and the physical, must be considered always in inter-

action. For this reason, we must map composition in terms of the exclusionary potential of spaces and see the potential for constructing alternative modes of access. ("Mapping" 16)

WPAs need to participate in this mapping of the spaces—like our program attendance policies—that may be creating impediments in our writing programs in order to reimagine ways to create more access.

Mandatory attendance (and tardiness) standards arguably serve the purpose of getting students to come to class on time, but they are grounded in ableist assumptions about the ease of waking to an alarm clock, getting out of bed, and making it to class in a timely manner (among others). For some students with disabilities, however, some or none of these things are easy assumptions. A student who has just changed medications may be unable to sleep at night, only to crash in the early morning hours and sleep right through her morning alarm. A student with fibromyalgia might be so weakened and sore that it is too painful for him to move. A student who uses a wheelchair might not be able to navigate the campus's icy sidewalks if the ground crew hasn't salted the paths yet. Should these students be penalized for missing class? Are their absences of the same kind as the absences of students who are too hungover to get out of bed or of students who simply don't want to come to class? Furthermore, how do we, teachers and administrators, decide who is worthy of exception to our policies? What makes us qualified to judge the conditions of others' lives, especially given composition studies' very prominent mission of social justice? Honestly, do we really want to continue in this adjudicative role?

An important first step in beginning to answer these questions is an awareness of the critical perspective disability studies scholarship brings to conversations about embodiment and disability. To oversimplify for the sake of explanation, disability scholars speak of two models of disability. The first is a biomedical model that anchors disability in the body via some diagnosable, locatable, medical condition, disease, or malfunction. For example, in the biomedical model of disability, a person who cannot walk is disabled because a spinal cord injury paralyzes her lower body; the paralysis is the disability. On the other hand, in the social model of disability, scholars argue that the built environment, not a medical condition, creates the condition of disability. Using the same example, then, we would say that a person who cannot walk is disabled only because she encounters material circumstances that limit her mobility. If buildings no longer had stairs, if all curbs had curb cuts, if cars had standard hand controls, etc., not being able to walk would not limit her mobility in any way; therefore, walking on two legs would just be one of many equally navigable mobility options. In the social model, then, disability is constructed by choices society makes about norms.[5]

The tensions between these two models of disability are very much in play in higher education where many institutional (not just writing program) policies are based on a biomedical model of disability. Yet, in colleges and universities, when the topic of disability comes up, the conversation inevitably turns to accessibility and accommodations, features of the constructed environment. Accessibility is usually about the built environment (ramps, stairs, elevators) while accommodation is about practices (timed tests, electronic devices, etc.) and "procedural changes and modifications in teaching and academic evaluation practices" (Jung 269). Both accessibility and accommodation mandates are needed because either the campus physical environment or the classroom (pedagogical) environment have been constructed (social) with the normate student in mind. For example, if all buildings had ramps, there would no need to move a class for a student using a wheelchair. If timed tests weren't used, students with processing disorders wouldn't need extra time. In this way, accessibility and accommodation mandates operate to address the concerns of the social model of disability.

However, the very process by which students activate their legal rights to access and accommodation is steeped in biomedical authorization. Consider the standard operating procedure at many institutions: To get accommodations under the ADA, students need to submit medical documentation to a designated person (usually a disability coordinator of some kind) who then certifies that the student 1) qualifies as disabled under the government sanctioned definitions of disability and 2) is permitted to have a certain set of reasonable accommodations. The determination of eligibility for disability accommodation can only be made if there is supporting, written documentation from some sort of institutional authority (a doctor, a therapist, a testing specialist). As teachers, we are made aware when this process occurs because students hand us official letters from the disability office telling us that they get time and a half on tests, or a distraction-free testing environment, or an in-class note-taker, etc.

The process by which students must obtain their legal rights to accommodations quickly turns the conversation away from what individual students need or want and instead turns the entire process into one about meeting legal standards and medical definitions of disability.[6] Perhaps even more harmfully, when we force students to get the imprimatur of the disability services office before we will offer them tools to allow them to be more successful in class, we are reinforcing the ideal of the normate student body. This reinscription of the ideal student makes accommodation about seeking favors and advantages. As Karen Jung reminds us, "the process of accommodation—which involves providing special exceptions to the ordinary rules—also contributes to the ableism that singles out disabled people as targets of resentment" (271). Having to be an exception, asking for an exemption, being a special case is not a desirable position to be in, yet, policies (and pedagogies) premised on ableism situate students with disabilities in precisely this position all the time. Cynthia Lewiecki-Wilson and Brenda Brueggeman point out that this positioning can have "dire academic consequences" as many college-aged students with disabilities will not even register with the disability office because of the stigma or simply because of the difficulties inherent in the process itself (2–4).

I believe so many FYW instructors come to me about our attendance policy because, even though they cannot articulate the reasons, they sense the inherent contradictions between compositions' emphasis on student empowerment and the ways that the mandatory attendance policy disempowers them. Our instructors want to help their students, not penalize them, yet the structures our writing program creates around attendance forces our instructors into a Catch-22: per their employment contract, instructors are required to uphold all writing program policies and procedures, yet, the writing program attendance policy simply does not work for all students because it is based on the normate student body. Our attendance policy creates the very conditions under which we need to make multiple exemptions. Our policy rhetorically constructs disabling situations for our students and our instructors.

Marking Difference

Because we have created the conditions under which we now operate, we have the power to change them. As James Porter et al. remind us:

> Though institutions are certainly powerful, they are not monoliths; they are rhetorically constructed human designs (whose power is reinforced by buildings, laws, traditions, and knowledge-making practices) and so are changeable. In other words, we made 'em, we can fix 'em. (611)

As the WPA, I am tasked with creating and maintaining my writing program's policies and procedures. Indeed, in a 2012 survey of WPAs and department chairs, Shirley Rose et al. discovered that creating, implementing, and maintaining writing program policy is a key component of many WPAs' jobs (57). Despite Porter et al.'s call to harness the rhetorical power of what we have created, however, WPAs have paid surprisingly little critical attention to how our program policies function as rhetorical constructs.[7]

For the remainder of this essay, then, I am going to explore some alternative pathways for re-thinking normate-centric policies. While I do not claim to have this all worked out, I hope to jumpstart critical, productive conversations about how our writing program policies do or do not welcome disability and invite us to brainstorm ways to adjust accordingly.

One way composition scholars are engaging with diversity, especially disability, is moving beyond what Stephanie Kerschbaum calls fixing difference, that is: "treating difference as a stable thing or property that can be identified and fixed in place" (*Toward* 6). Fixing difference maps on to the biomedical model of disability in that fixing difference involves choosing certain qualities or characteristics—race, class, gender, dis/ability—and assigning a person to that category as the sole determinant of their identity and marker of difference. For example, labeling Tighe as disabled would be fixing Tighe in the category of disabled, eliding all the other things about Tighe that make him who he is. Like the biomedical model that always points to identifiable, label-able causes for disability, fixing difference always points to a particular characteristic or quality that makes someone different from someone else in a static way.

Writing program policies, by their very nature, are primed to fix difference precisely because they function to standardize experience across multiple sections of what is supposed to be the same course. Fixing difference in program policy leads to the scenarios that began this essay. Because our attendance policy is written for normate students—students who will not have major depressive episodes as Leandra might be having, students who will not have trouble navigating campus as Tighe might be having, or even students like Jasmine whom we know little about—our teachers are left with three choices, none of them optimal: 1) subject themselves to reprimand for not following writing program rules by not docking Leandra's, Tighe's, and Jasmine's grades; 2) subject their students to lower grades for breaking writing program rules (after three absences. . .) or 3) attempt to find ways to make exceptions for their students who don't seem to fit neatly under the rules as they are written. Our students are left to either ask for an exception to be made, to other themselves from their classmates, or to accept a lower grade for circumstances that may be out of their control.

While it is tempting at this point to say we should just eliminate attendance policies, this solution is not practical. Policies are necessary aids to ensuring all students receive equitable treatment. When I was an associate dean overseeing grade appeals, incomplete requests, and authorizing late withdraws from classes, I frequently turned to college policy for guidance in order to confirm that I was not giving one student a special consideration I was not giving another. This doesn't mean I didn't take individual circumstances into account—I considered it my duty to make informed, ethical decisions based on coordination between college policy and the particularities of each student's situation. But I definitely needed and wanted a general statement of the beliefs and desires of the college regarding the issues I was asked to decide on. We need writing program policies for these same reasons. Instead of eschewing policy completely, we need to find a new way—a broader way—to envision what our policies can do.

Kerschbaum suggests just such an approach. Instead of fixing—or fixating—on difference, she asks us to mark difference, a rhetorical move that encourages us not to erase the reality of differences nor elide those differences. Marking difference creates space for constantly shifting identities to be reconstituted and reconstructed *kairotically.* The process of marking difference allows for fluidity and negotiation in every relationship (*Toward* 7; 67). Marking difference easily maps on to the social model of disability because marking difference is about situatedness. Returning to Tighe's situation, then, we might say that Tighe is disabled when it comes to getting across campus, but when he is playing basketball in his wheelchair league, the category of disabled no longer holds any relevance; when he is playing basketball, Tighe most strongly identifies as a forward. When we mark difference, we use a rhetorical lens that "emphasizes the relationship between speaker/writer [writing program policy] and audience [students] as well as the situated nature of all communicative activity" (*Toward* 67). This *kairotic* process of marking difference seems especially apt for the writing classroom as teachers and students often have a chance to build personal relationships because of our relatively small class sizes and the give-and-take of the writing process. If our policies were constructed with the intention of marking instead of fixing difference, our rules might not be so rigid and formulaic, and a wide range of attendance policies could be on the table.

The moment of critical intervention for WPAs comes precisely at this point where the need for policy, a need that strongly pulls us towards fixation, begs for a reality that allows for the fluidity of marking difference. But creating these kinds of policies is no easy task. Kerschbaum herself admits that

> It still sometimes makes me anxious when students ask me to allow or excuse a large number of absences. [. . .]. It is never simple for me to figure out how to fully reconcile my belief that it is valuable for students to engage with me and their classmates during class meetings with the fact that some students are not always able to be physically present for those sessions. ("Anecdotal" n. pag.)

Besides working through our own personal and pedagogical desires for students to be physically present at all time in our classrooms, reimagining our program policies raises two other salient issues: How do WPAs make policy decisions that focus on what individual students and teachers might need, yet, at the same time, have these policies perform the necessary work of structuring common program expectations and requirements? If we are able to create fluid program policies, how do we enforce them in equitable ways?

UNIVERSAL DESIGN FOR POLICY-MAKING

In a recent conference paper, subtitled "Throw Away Your Attendance Policy: For the Love of God Do it Now," Catherine Prendergast explains that she has experimented with cripping her attendance policy for students who cannot always make it to class because of some disability they have disclosed to her. "Cripping," in this case, means "throwing it away." For Prendergast, "To 'crip' our attendance policy, we must recognize that there will be no conformity to a norm, whether a norm of disability or a norm of ability. We stop enabling a systemic erasure of [students'] disabilities" (9). As a classroom teacher, I admit that I, too, have thrown away my attendance policy. Some instructors fear that if they don't have a mandatory attendance policy, students will miss more class. Prendergast reports anecdotally, and my own anecdotal evidence echoes hers, that the absence of a mandatory attendance policy does not negatively impact attendance.[8] Cripping our attendance policies might be one way that individual teachers can avoid fixating on difference on their own syllabi; however, I'm not so certain the cripping of attendance policies by throwing them out can be scaled up to the programmatic level.

As I argued above, program policies do serve the important function of ensuring that students are held to similar expectations and receive similar experiences across multiple sections of the same course. Similar, however, does not mean the same, so we do not need to continue with overly prescriptive policies (after three absences. . .). Instead, maybe we can start incorporating the concepts of Universal Design (UD) into our policy-making. UD, or UDL (Universal Design for Learning) is a pedagogical model developed by disability educators.[9] Lewiecki-Wilson and Brueggemann remind us that "the *universal* in UDL means that one should design a class in anticipation of a variety of student learners, not for a single type of universal, idealized, abstract student" (6; emphasis original). While UD is classroom focused, its principles can be easily applied to policy making; we should create policy for a variety of students, not a normate student. This call for universality clearly resonates with Kerschbaum's call to mark difference. Both UD and marking difference are premised on the interactions among teachers, students, and the environment.

Here is my very modest proposal. Let's flip the script and ground writing program policies in a non-normative perspective. Using our attendance policy as an example, let's say that instead of assuming getting to class every day on time is a simple task, let's start from the assumption that students, like their professors, have complicated lives and bodies that will never reach the Platonic ideal. Based on this common understanding of embodiment, the three-strikes-and-you-are-out versions of attendance policies no longer seem just. Let's stop penalizing students for their bodies not being in the classroom space and instead focus more on ways to make the classroom space more fluid. Let's find ways to make attendance an honest and open negotiation among stakeholders. As Dolmage reminds us, "UD is not a tailoring of the environment to marginal groups; it is a form of hope, a manner of trying" ("Mapping" 24).

If our writing program rewrites our attendance policy to empower instructors to work with their students, to start from a collaborative space instead of a regulatory or punitive space Leandra, Tighe, and Jasmine, as well as their classmates, would have the chance to freely negotiate with their instructors. Their instructors would not have to fear a reprimand for not following writing program policy, and the students would not be made to feel as though they were asking for special treatment, nor would they need to necessarily come out in an official way by registering with the disability services' office. Finally, the idea of exceptions would all but disappear as all attendance matters, for all students, would be open for discussion. I do not yet know how to capture this desire in a program policy; I have not yet found the right words to create an effective non-mandatory writing program attendance policy, but I am hopeful, and I invite other WPAs to join me in trying.

NOTES

1. The scenarios presented in this essay are based on actual situations I have encountered as a WPA and Associate Dean overseeing disability services; however, I have taken liberties with the details of each vignette for the sake of brevity and narrative coherence.

2. While not explicitly stated in our policy, lore in our program has made the "three tardies equals one absence" standard a de facto policy.

3. I use "student body" here to refer to both a singular body and the collective.

4. These assumptions are hiding in some of our pedagogical practices, too; however, that discussion is beyond the scope of this essay.

5. Within disability studies, there is debate about how to describe the construction of non-physical, chronic, and/or invisible disabilities like mental illness, fibromyalgia, chronic pain, cancer, etc. For highly nuanced discussions of these topics see Davis; Price, Siebers.

6. I want to pause here and shout out that I concur with Jung who has rightly pointed out that accommodations have allowed many, many students who were previously denied a college education access to the academy. For that reason alone, access and accommodations are worth celebrating. Also see Lewiecki-Wilson and Brueggemann.

7. There is evidence that disability scholars in composition are starting to make this turn toward policy discussions. Wood and Madden, for an example, perform a rhetorical analysis of how disability accommodation statements are presented on syllabi and Vidali offers and embodied theory of plagiarism.

8. Obviously the field would benefit from a formal study of what happens to student attendance in the absence of mandatory attendance policies.

9. A special thank you to Catherine Prendergast for pointing out that the vision I was describing for policy-making was in line with the principles of UD.

Appendix A: University XXXX Core Writing Program Handbook

According to XXX policy, there are no excused absences (see "Class Absences" in XXX's course catalog). Attendance is particularly important in Core Writing courses because so much of the learning in these courses happens during in-class writing exercises, peer review, and discussion. Nevertheless, students are allowed [two absences without penalty if course meets two days per week; three days if course meets three days per week]. Every absence thereafter will result in a penalty to your course grade; after [four (for a twice-weekly course) or six (for a thrice-weekly course)] absences, you will be failed from the course for excessive absences.

There are a very few exceptions to this policy. One is if you are representing the university in an official capacity (sports, debate, band, etc.). In this case you *may* qualify for a limited number of additional absences. To qualify for this exemption, you must bring me official notification (on university letterhead, complete with contact information) from a university official by the end of the second week in class. Once I have your letter, you and I will decide if you should remain in the course or should find a section whose schedule better fits yours. The other exception may come in case of serious injury/illness. If you wish to petition for an additional limited number of absences, you or a representative must notify me within a week of the incident. Again, there are no excused absences from XXX courses, so exceptions are at my discretion and must be negotiated by the above conditions.

If you miss a class, it is your duty to determine what you have missed. As for tardiness, you need to be in your seat when class starts and ends. If you are not, I reserve the right to mark you absent.

WORKS CITED

Davis, Lennard. *The End of Normal: Identity in a Biocultural Era*. U of Michigan P, 2013.

Dolmage, Jay. "Mapping Composition: Inviting Disability in the Front Door." *Disability and the Teaching of Writing: A Critical Sourcebook*, edited by Cynthia Lewiecki-Wilson and Brenda Brueggemann. Bedford/St. Martin's, 2008, pp. 14–27.

—. "Writing Against Normal: Navigating a Corporeal Turn." *composing(media) =composing(embodiment): bodies, technologies, writing, the teaching of writing*, edited by Kristin Arola and Anne Frances Wysocki. Utah State UP, 2012, pp. 110–26.

Dolmage, Jay, and Cynthia Lewiecki-Wilson. "Refiguring Rhetorica: Linking Feminist Rhetoric and Disability Studies." *Rhetorica in Motion: Feminist Rhetorical Methods and Methodologies*, edited by Eileen Schell and K. J. Rawson. University of Pittsburgh Press, 2010, pp. 23–38.

Jung, Karen Elizabeth. "Chronic Illness and Educational Equity: The Politics of Visibility." *Feminist Disability Studies*, edited by Kim Q. Hall. Indiana UP, 2011, pp. 263–86.

Kerschbaum, Stephanie. "Anecdotal Relations: On Orienting to Disability in the Composition Classroom." *Composition Forum*, vol. 32, 2015, compositionforum.com/issue/32/anecdotal-relations.php. Accessed 10 June 2016.

—. *Toward a New Rhetoric of Difference*. CCCC/NCTE, 2014.

Lewiecki-Wilson, Cynthia and Brenda Brueggemann. "Rethinking Practices and Pedagogy: Disability and the Teaching of Writing." *Disability and the Teaching of Writing: A Critical Sourcebook*, edited by Cynthia Lewiecki-Wilson and Brenda Brueggemann. Bedford/St. Martin's, 2008, pp. 1–9.

Porter, James, Patricia Sullivan, Stuart Blythe, Jeffrey T. Grabill, and \Libby Miles. "Institutional Critique: A Rhetorical Methodology for Change" *College Composition and Communication* vol. 51, no. 4, 2000, pp. 610–42.

Prendergast, Catherine. "Ableism and Attendance: Making the Writing Classroom Accessible to All Students." NEMLA Convention. Baltimore Marriott Waterfront, Hartford, CT. 18 March 2016.

Price, Margaret. *Mad at School: Rhetorics of Mental Disability and Academic Life*. University of Michigan Press, 2011.

Rose, Shirley K, Lisa Mastrangelo, and Barbara L'Eplattenier. "Directing First-Year Writing: The New Limits of Authority." *College Composition and Communication* vol. 65, no. 1, 2013, pp. 43–66.

Siebers, Tobin. *Disability Theory*. U of Michigan P, 2011.

University of Nevada, Reno. *Core Writing Program Handbook* 2015–2016.

Vidali, Amy. "Embodying/Disabling Plagiarism." *JAC* vol. 31, no.1/2, 2011, pp. 248–66.

Wood, Tara and Shannon Madden. "Suggested Practices for Syllabus Accessibility Statements." *Kairos: A Journal of Rhetoric, Technology, and Pedagogy* vol.18, no. 1, 2013, www/jstor.org/stable/20866995. Accessed 15 July 2016.

Melissa Nicolas is Associate Dean of Undergraduate Education and Director of the Merritt Writing Program at UC Merced. She is also co-chair of the CWPA Mentoring Project. She is editor/co-editor of two collections and the author of numerous articles and book chapters. Continuing the work of this article, she is currently working on a qualitative study of the effect of attendance policies on student attendance.

Toward Inclusive and Multi-Method Writing Assessment for College Students with Learning Disabilities: The (Universal) Story of Max

Steven J. Corbett

Abstract

This essay draws on current research on learning disabilities (LDs) and writing pedagogy, writing assessment scholarship, and my own case study research to explore options for an inclusive, multi-method model of writing assessment with and for LD students. I highlight the experiences of one student writer (self-identified as autistic) in particular: Max. In the first part, I engage concepts of Universal Design for Learning (UDL), and arguments involving connections between LD and basic writing students. In the second part, I detail how peer-to-peer and portfolio pedagogies can enact principles of UDL for all student writers. In part three, I offer multivoiced case study research with Max and two other course-based tutoring participants: his instructor, Mya, and the tutor, Sara (self-identified as dyslexic). I describe the interactions of all three participants as they worked together and with other students in a developmental first-year writing classroom. I also touch on the subsequent collaborative activities we undertook together, including presenting our work at local and regional conferences. In the final part, I offer four principles for building and sustaining inclusive assessment mechanisms for LD and—by design—all student writers.

> *Hello everyone! My name is Max, and I'm a junior majoring in Accounting at X State University in X. To tell you a little about myself, I was born with autism, obsessive compulsive disorder, and anxiety. Autism presents challenges with speech and language and, due to my having this disability, I have always struggled with comprehension and writing in school. When I was in grammar school, I could not even write one para-*

graph if I did not have total guidance from my parents and my teachers. I always felt very vulnerable because of my disability, but liked school and was determined to go to college.

Max, a student with high-functioning autism, expressed these opening words aloud eloquently and passionately in our panel at a 2012 regional writing center conference. Let's juxtapose Max's personal sentiments (which readers will hear more of throughout this article) to some broader statistics regarding students with learning disabilities (LDs):

- According to Boyle et al., "Developmental disabilities are common and were reported in 1 in 6 children in the United States in 2006-2008. The number of children with select developmental disabilities (autism, attention deficit hyperactivity disorder, and other developmental delays) has increased from [12.84% to 15.04% over 12 years], requiring more health and education services" (1034).
- Shannon Walters reports that "Directors of Student Disability Services at two major universities estimate that only half of students with disabilities report their disabilities and note that students with disabilities often forgo accommodations for which they are eligible because they believe their instructors will treat them differently" (427).

During a case study of course-based tutoring in a developmental writing course at a four-year comprehensive state university, I came to know Max well. My involvement with him, his peer tutor Sara (who also identified as having an LD, dyslexia), and their instructor, Mya, led me to investigate disability studies theory and research. I soon found myself confronting the question of what is the best sort of learning environment for student writers with LDs. Like Amy Vidali, Margaret Price, and Cynthia Lewiecki-Wilson—editors of the 2008 special issue of *Disability Studies Quarterly* "Disability Studies in the Undergraduate Classroom"—I became concerned with questions of how higher education is welcoming these students and how we might work toward designing more accommodating conditions for neurodiverse students, accommodations that—by design—might also benefit all students, teachers, and writing programs. Like Vidali in her 2015 *WPA* essay "Disabling Writing Program Administration," I wanted to attempt "the challenge of disabling WPA narratives," in order to "invite disability in new and diverse ways" (47) in relation to discussions of writing assessment.

While there is a substantial amount of literature on ideal learning environments for student writers with LDs, and recent writing assessment scholarship urges principles of multi-method and inclusive design (see, for example, White et al. 142-68; Inoue, *Antiracist* 283-300), all instructors of writing could benefit from more explicit discussions of how these two issues intersect. In other words, how might the needs of LD students fit within current writing assessment designs and practices? The following multi-voiced study offers WPAs a framework for designing inclusive, multi-method models of assessment for LD student writers. This framework is based on working toward two universal goals: 1) first and foremost, the idea of universal acceptance and 2) the idea of universal accommodation. Specifically, I describe an assessment frame that includes mainstreaming LD students, a focus on peer-to-peer and ePortfolio collaborative performances, and multi-method measures that include student self-representation. Following Patricia Dunn's exhortation that "Young people's versions of their experiences should be just as valid as the version given by the most credentialed among us" (97), and in the spirit of the disability rights movement motto "Nothing About Us Without Us," I relay the story of Max via case study research with other course-based tutoring participants, his instructor Mya, and his peer tutor Sara. I represent their collaborations—in their own words as much as possible—as they worked together and with other students in the developmental writing classroom. I hope to ultimately offer fellow instructors and WPAs suggestions for ways we can continue to work with like-minded thinkers to build more inclusive assessment mechanisms for LD (and all) student writers.

Why Design for Inclusive and Universal Assessment?

My first year experience at college was nerve-wracking at first mainly because I had no idea what to expect. I felt fairly confident that I could hold my own in the mathematical courses, but I worried about how I would survive the challenges of the English courses I would need to take to graduate. Math came easy to me as it is very concrete: there is always a right or wrong answer. English was another story altogether. There were many questions that I had in my head: Would I be able to keep up with the rest of the class? Would I get confused about the directions for assignments? Would I understand the material in order to write appropriate responses?

Fortunately, I was placed in a remedial English course to better prepare me to handle the challenges of the required English courses I would need to eventually take. Having the opportunity to be a student in this course was an important stepping stone for me to work on my language and comprehension skills with reading and writing. At the point that I began college, I was able to organize my thoughts better and understand that sometimes things are not always concrete. But I had a long way to go. I still depend greatly on other people to help me, and I needed to gain confidence in myself. I wanted to work on developing my thoughts and ideas in an organized manner. I wanted to become a better writer. . .

What are some ways we—as teachers and administrators—can work toward attitudes and methods that embrace universal acceptance and design? And why should we? Like Max, so many students come to college with their fair share of anxiety and trepidation: returning, non-traditional students; students with social anxiety; students who have been labeled remedial or basic in their math or writing skills. Writing studies scholars have been thinking about these questions in terms of accommodating the many faces of student learning and performance ability, and several—from a variety of angles, including professional and technical communications (Greenbaum; Walters) and writing center theory and practice (Kiedaisch and Dinitz; Mann; Brizee et al.; Babcock and Daniels)—have answered by advocating theories and principles of universal design. The Center for Universal Design explains that its intent "is to simplify life for everyone by making products, communications, and the built environment more usable by as many people as possible at little or no extra cost. Universal design benefits people of all ages and abilities." Further, Universal Design for Learning (UDL) attempts to design curriculum that accommodate as many people as possible, while still pushing against a one-size-fits-all pedagogical solution. Several of the elements of their comprehensive accommodation frame feature pedagogical methods and strategies familiar to writing studies, including

- teaching for transfer;
- developing cognitive and motivational scaffolds;
- designing multiple forms of performance modeling, mentoring, and feedback in problem-exploring situations;
- fostering peer-to-peer collaboration and support; and
- providing options for self-regulation, self-assessment, and reflection. (National Center on Universal Design for Learning).

The developmental writing classroom, like the one Max found himself placed into, is a pedagogical location where this sort of balanced, multi-dimensional philosophy makes sense to think more about.

But, starting with an often crucial first question in writing assessment, should students with LDs be placed in typical developmental writing classrooms in the first place? Kimber Barber-Fendley and Chris Hamel argue that it is impossible to establish a neutral or equal playing field for LD students in the writing classroom. Instead, they propose alternate assistance programs that provide supplemental instructional resources outside of class. They argue that supplemental instruction conducted outside of the classroom can better support LD students' privacy and dignity. However, disability scholars like Vidali and Mark Mossman disagree. Vidali urges us to do what we can to unify basic writing and LD pedagogies in the same classrooms ("Discourses"). She believes that LD students have much in common with more traditional basic writing students (including that they are both overcoming some sort of learning deficit that labels them as other) and benefit from the structural support systems afforded basic writers in all their various diversities. This integrative attitude echoes Mossman's belief that, for LD students, classroom environments need to be places where they can claim power and equality through what he posits as a process of "authentification." This process occurs, Mossman explains,

> when disability is understood as 'normal,' and in our classrooms this process of normalization happens only when we allow our students, all of them, to speak, to fully participate in the discussion, when we give them, all of them, a normalized status. (656; also see Dunn, 110; 163-64)

Universal acceptance, like the type called for by (self-identified) autistic scholars Scott Robertson and Ari Ne'eman, starts with deep listening for what makes LD students unique, as well as what pedagogical methods and assessment mechanisms might work toward authentification and inclusivity. Taking steps toward universal accommodation means engaging all students in aspects of personal and social development via writing practices that cultivate deep meaning-making activities through clear writing expectations and interactive writing processes (Anderson et al.). Two commonly used pedagogical tools in writing classrooms—peer-to-peer collaboration and ePortfolios—can be combined to help writing instructors work toward universal acceptance and accommodation, for all students.

Two Tools for Universal Learning Assessment: Peer-to-Peer Pedagogies and ePortfolios

One of the best features of my introductory English course was the built-in support system that was available to me. It was a small class, and my professor was able to give all of us individualized assistance. In addition, the class had a peer tutor who was always available to help me. My tutor helped alleviate my anxiety over the understanding of assignments, as she would go over the specifics with me before I started it. She gave me ideas and examples to consider when I worked on my essays. I learned to use an

> *online site for creating my writing portfolio. My teacher and peer tutor*
> *were able to monitor my work on the site and give me the important feed-*
> *back I needed in order to improve my writing.*

Whether intended for LD or able-for-now students, strong currents in writing studies have flowed toward the adoption of peer-to-peer (including peer review and response, writing center, and writing fellow) and portfolio pedagogies as strategies for accommodating a wide array of student learners. The complex relationship between how students perceive what it means to write at the college level and how instructors go about facilitating this learning has led writing studies scholars for the past thirty years to link the importance of reflective and metacognitive practice to writing assessment, especially holistic assessment (Yancey; Huot and O'Neill; Carroll 120–26). Composition scholars have further linked the importance of reflective and metacognitive practice to portfolio assessment (Yancey; Huot and O'Neill; Wills and Rice; White and Wright; Yancey et al.; Condon et al. 45-71). Kathleen Yancey's extensive portfolio and ePortfolio research maintains that writing portfolios are exercises in substantial reflective activity. She further links reflection to identity formation or formation of the self. She writes, "The self provides a lens through which we can look backward and forward at once, to inquire as to how it was constructed . . .The self is constructed quite explicitly through reflection" (498-99; 500). If we continue to help all students (and ourselves) think of the reflective process as the creative and critical exploration of the self through writing, through time and attention, we will enable students to simultaneously look back to their former selves while looking forward to their potential selves. It will also enable a more creative and critical presentation of those potential selves to the assessment world of multiple readers and audiences.

Among the questions that portfolio assessments enable us to ask, then, like what, how, and why am I supposed to be learning here, the question of with and from who am I learning—or the question of models—is an important concept for designing inclusive writing assessments. Social learning theory, including five decades of pioneering research by Albert Bandura, posits that students acquire much information about their capabilities through knowledge of how others perform. Things like goal achievement and motivation are affected when students perceive their performances as either similar to or significantly different from others. Students will attend to models when they believe the modeled tasks will help them achieve their goals. One interesting connection between peer-to-peer pedagogies and metacognition is the idea of coping and mastery peer models (Bransford et al. 67, 279; Carroll 136-37; compare to Condon et al. 92-113). Coping models initially demonstrate the typical fears and deficiencies of observers but gradually improve their performance and gain confidence in their capabilities. Mastery models exhibit high confidence and flawless performance from the outset. In order to learn from models, students need to see a variety of performers, with different modeling styles. A diversity of models might also address students' various learning styles and predilections. Modeling for universal learning would involve not only providing a writing environment where motivation-enhancing short-term goals are explicitly built into lessons and chances to view both coping and mastery models abound, but would also encourage students to reflect on their collaborative experiences.

EQUITABLE ASSESSMENT IN ACTION

> *Many times our class was broken up into groups, and through peer editing, we were able to learn from each other's strengths and weaknesses. We supported each other, and I began to get involved in class discussions because I knew no one would ridicule me. I was okay with making mistakes, as I knew I would be guided in how to correct them. When I did not understand something, my professor and tutor would patiently explain the material to me. My fears lessened as my confidence grew, and I took more chances with my writing—which was a big step for me.*

During my case study research with Max and his classmates, his tutor (Sara), and his instructor (Mya), I witnessed peer-to-peer and ePortfolio pedagogies intertwining in compelling ways. The first time I visited the class to observe participant interactions during peer review and response, I noticed Max visibly struggling. His two peer group partners seemed to be experiencing no trouble at all. The peer tutor, Sara, who was circulating around the room, saw that Max was having trouble. She later said:

> I noticed Max looking nervous over in his seat so I went over to see what I could help him with. His partners Kim and Adrianne already had their computers set up and were starting the assignment. Max wasn't as far along. He hadn't even logged into the computer.

Sara spent much of the remaining class session helping him get on track with the multiple complex organizational and communicative tasks students needed to negotiate during this peer review and response session: working with online files, following the response guidelines and instructions, and reading and offering feedback to his group members.

During my second visit, just one month later, I noticed both Max and his peer response partners taking on much more interactive collaborative roles. Max seemed in much better shape—no visible worries. I noticed that rather than frequently asking Sara for help, he seemed to be much more involved with his two partners. In contrast to what I witnessed during my earlier visit, Max seemed to have a good grasp of what he was supposed to be doing. He asked his partners a question and they helped him; they asked him questions and he helped them. I was impressed with how well all three students in Max's group were communicating and interacting. In contrast to my last visit, Sara only came over to the group a couple of times. At one point, the group talked about works cited pages and the fact that neither of Max's partners did one, but that he did. Sara ended up spending much more focused time with other students, including a male student who was having difficulty with citations and formatting. Sara gave her impressions of her involvement with Max and his group members in this second peer review session: "I looked at Max's work and realized he was very ahead of the game. He had his ePortfolio set up very nicely. He already had one paper posted and was almost ready to post another."

By the time I interviewed Max near the end of the term, I found out much more about his personal and social journey as an autistic student, a journey that whispered the importance of inclusive writing assessments. He spoke of specific teachers he felt were rude and disrespectful: a "crazy" sixth grade teacher in the resource room who would yell at him; a history teacher in his sophomore year of high school who was "ignorant of him and not a very nice person" and, in addition to being mean and rude to everyone else in the class, (Max would find out) he made fun of Max outside of class. When reminded of just how emotionally challenging school can be for all students, the importance of working toward universal acceptance in attitude and action becomes paramount.

Max went on to say that he has trouble with writing prompts and does not do well with standardized tests like the SAT. He said that he does not think it is fair that students with LDs have to take and pass those tests. He feels, rather, that they are far too time consuming and that a better indication of any student's intelligence is how hard they work. Regarding the SAT and ACT, he said, "It's hurting a lot of people, especially those with learning disabilities." He feels that in college he is better able to advocate for himself; he has become more independent, and only relies on the campus Disability Resource Center for paperwork to give to his instructors asking for extended times for test taking. He said he was given the option by Mya to move from English 110 on to English 112, but he chose to go to the intermediary English 111 instead because he wants to eventually "kick butt in English 112!" He said that while he feels he is getting much stronger on so many things with his writing, he believes all the constant practice with planning and revising is making him so much better. During our interview, Mya emphasized this important point:

> By the end of the course described above, Max proved to be the most successful student in the class and was deemed ready by several teachers/readers [during end-of-term portfolio norming sessions] of his work to be offered the chance to skip a level. This is huge, I think, since only about two to four [English] 110 students per semester are invited to do so. And he came from so far behind, at least in confidence, that semester.

Max's words regarding the inequity of standardized tests versus the sort of meaningful assessment he experienced in his first-year composition courses, underscores the importance of universal accommodation in writing assessment design. Vidali et al., reflecting on their *DSQ* special issue, found it somewhat disconcerting how often they received submissions describing traditional instructional practices like timed-writing, lecture-based class formats, and heavy reading and writing loads. This led them to a qualified lament: "While the presence of disability 'curricula' or 'content' in so many locations is impressive, the adoption of inclusive *pedagogies* appears less common" (also see Greenbaum 41).

Max's peer tutor, Sara, told me about the class's end-of-term party. It stands in stark contrast to the first time I saw Max struggling in the classroom:

> Today we had a party for our last day of class . . .It was amazing to see Max interacting with all the students. They were including him in the conversation and you could hear the joy in his voice. I thought this was amazing because Max had been very uptight and nervous for the first part of the semester. This class has been so accepting of him, so he finally started letting a little loose. After one class about half way through the semester I was talking to Max after class and he told me that college was so much nicer than high school; the people are so nice. I got the impression that Max's high school was not very accepting of him, so it was great that Max got to interact with a wonderful group of students. As class came to an end, each student said goodbye to all the other students. It was a great end to the wonderful semester with these students.

What if we could give every student—as much as possible—such experiences to associate with writing, as they move through their time in college, as they look back from their professional lives? What if assessment systems were designed with a single universal-as-possible student like Max at the center, as the gravity that all other parts of the system orbited around? We might see a system of universal social imbrication and support like the one represented in figure 1.

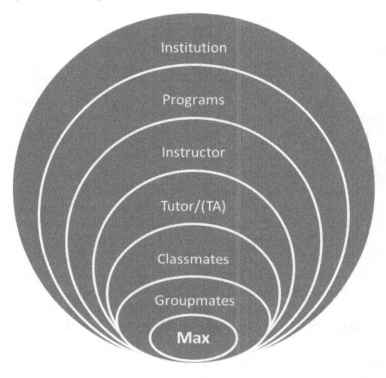

Figure 1. System of universal social imbrication for equitable assessment

I came to reflect on what I was observing and hearing with Max and his colleagues as very much in line with a universal design for learning philosophy. In her mediations on the accommodation of autistic students in the writing center, April Mann relates how writing center studies has had to come to terms with some pedagogical beliefs about student autonomy and teacher control and directiveness, instances where "tutors working with students with [autism spectrum] sounds very similar to best practices advice for writing teachers and tutors in general. The difference," she found, lying "in how much help students might need, not in the type of help they might need" (53). The types of recursive, multi-dimensional writing situations Max experienced in his developmental writing course exemplified this universally inclusive emphasis on "how much" rather than "type." In the end, I believe the collaborative learning environment established by the close instructional partnership between Mya and Sara enabled *all* students in their basic writing course to experience learning to write and writing-to-learn at an optimal level. Further, the collaborative research process—including conference presentations like the one delivered throughout this article by Max—in which all participants engaged added another important metacognitive learning level. Since all participants were interviewed and followed up with in depth, gathered together to reflect on their experiences as a group, and were involved in the textual interpretation and analysis of the data presented, all participants experienced multiple learning moments in relation to the overall case study. Over the course of seven years, all participants have had an active and dialogical role in their own self-representation.

PRINCIPLED SUGGESTIONS FOR DESIGNING INCLUSIVE WRITING ASSESSMENTS

> *I think one of the best benefits of my intro to English class was that I found I actually liked English. I enjoyed reading and discussing the material the most, but even the part I always feared,* writing, *became more enjoyable. I felt a sense of pride and accomplishment when I would write something and receive positive feedback from my professor. Writing will always remain my biggest challenge, but I have come a long way, and I feel confident that I will continue to grow.*

Scholars in WAC and their disciplinary partners have reported success in developing cross-curricular cohorts that closely collaborate in efforts to design effective writing assessments (Broad et al.; Yancey et al.; Anson et al.; Soliday; White et al.). When students work closely with other students, and their writing process and product performances are delivered via ePortfolio, they are enacting a similar collaborative network of enterprise: holding a stake in, engaging in, and contributing to the mechanisms of their own assessment. Throughout this little essay, my colleagues and I have tried to offer some of the implications of why we should continue to think conscientiously about designing for universal acceptance and accommodation. I'd like to end with four principles for ways we can continue to work with like-minded thinkers to design more inclusive assessment mechanisms for LD—and, in the process, all—student writers.

Principle 1

Assessment loops must begin with the valuing of student input that (for programs that use it) directed self-placement (DSP) can provide, and include mainstreaming of LD (Vidali; Mossman) students as much as possible. Recall how Max performed so strongly in his developmental English

110 class that he was deemed by Mya and other readers of his portfolio ready to move directly from English 110 into English 112. Yet he chose to go to the intermediary English 111. I believe his collaborative and reflective experiences in English 110 made him much more metacognitively aware of the probable value of taking that intermediary English 111 course. Max felt he could benefit from more practice, more time, and more thoughtful cognitive and motivational scaffolding (Mackiewicz and Thompson) that would support his desire to "kick butt in English 112!"

Principle 2

Assessment must be performance or "labor" focused (Inoue "Grade-Less;" "Teaching"; *Antiracist*). This includes prioritizing the *Framework for Success in Postsecondary Writing* "habits of mind" while coaching students toward the sorts of performance outcomes we might desire in writing assessments (White et al.) Recall, during my interview with Max he described what he felt was the undue stress placed upon him in high school by standardized tests. He feels that they are far too time consuming and that a better indication of any student's intelligence is how hard they work. The SAT and ACT, he said, are "hurting a lot of people, especially those with learning disabilities." Assessment mechanisms like (e)portfolios allow for much more equitable learning environments for all students, providing them—and instructors, and programs—with the time and space needed for optimum learning, development, and reflection (see Condon et al.).

Principle 3

Assessment must be multi-method, including self-assessment measures and (continuing from DSP) with inclusion of student voices/stories (Dunn; Lewiecki-Wilson and Brueggemann; Hobgood). Students should be considered major stakeholders in assessment loops, stakeholders—like Max and his tutor Sara—whose points of view are as equally valid and reliable as other assessment measures.

Principle 4

Assessment mechanisms must ask: How well are we facilitating LD students' personal and social development (Anderson et al.) and preparing them for life after college (MacNeil)? In order to do this and effectively gauge the progress of individual students, as well as to what degree programs are meeting the needs of these students, assessment must be (a) collaborative, socializing students through activities like guided peer review and response; and (b) longitudinal, scaffolding recursive pedagogical processes that facilitate self-regulation through delivery mechanisms like ePortfolios and meaningful mentorship experiences.

On that longitudinal note, I'd like to end this essay with where we began, the words of Max from the latest email reply I received from him:

> Dear Dr. Corbett,
>
> I want to say hello and wish you a Happy Holiday & Happy New Year! I read the story that you wrote and I really liked it. I'm forever honored for being part of your research. I learned a lot from you, Professor [Mya] & Sara. I wouldn't be as successful as I am today without all of your help.
>
> In the spring of 2014, I graduated from X State U cum laude with a 3.63 GPA. I'm currently working as a Finance Clerk in the Accounting Department at City Hall. I really like the people I work with. I never thought that I would be working for my hometown. I hope everything is well with your job and that the new year goes well.
>
> Sincerely,
> Max

Works Cited

Anderson, Paul, Chris M. Anson, Robert M. Gonyea, and Charles Paine. "The Contributions of Writing to Learning and Development: Results from a Large-Scale Multi-Institutional Study." *Research in the Teaching of English*, vol. 50, no. 2, Nov. 2015, pp. 199–235.

Anson, Chris M., Deanna P. Dannels, Pamela Flash, and Amy L. Housley Gaffney. "Big Rubrics and Weird Genres: The Futility of Using Generic Assessment Tools across Diverse Instructional Contexts." *The Journal of Writing Assessment*, vol. 5, no. 1, 2012, www.journalofwritingassessment.org/article.php?article=57.

Babcock, Rebecca Day, and Sharifa Daniels, editors. *Writing Centers and Disability*. Fountainhead P, forthcoming.

Barber-Fendley, Kimber, and Chris Hamel. "A New Visibility: An Argument for Alternative Assistance Programs for Students with Learning Disabilities." *College Composition and Communication*, vol. 55, no. 3, 2004, pp. 504–35.

Boyle, Coleen A., Sheree Boulet, Laura A. Schieve, Robin A. Cohen, Stephen J. Blumberg, Marshalyn Yeargin-Allsopp, Susanna Visser, and Michael D. Kogan "Trends in the Prevalence of Developmental Disabilities in US Children, 1997–2008." *Pediatrics*, vol. 127, no. 6, 2011, pp. 1034–42.

Bransford, John D., Ann L. Brown, and Rodney R. Cocking, editors. *How People Learn: Brain, Mind, Experience, and School*. National Academy P, 2000.

Brizee, Allen, Morgan Sousa, and Dana Lynn Driscoll. "Writing Centers and Students with Disabilities: The User-Centered Approach, Participatory Design, and Empirical Research as Collaborative Methodologies." *Computers and Composition*, vol. 29, no. 4, Dec. 2012, pp. 341–66.

Broad, Bob, Linda Adler-Kassner, Barry Alford, Jane Detweiler, Heidi Estrem, Susanmarie Harrington, Maureen McBride, Eric Stalions, and Scott Weeden *Organic Writing Assessment: Dynamic Criteria Mapping in Action*. Utah State UP, 2009.

Carroll, Lee Ann. *Rehearsing New Roles: How College Students Develop as Writers*. Southern Illinois UP, 2002.

The Center for Universal Design. University of North Carolina. www.ncsu.edu/ ncsu/design/cud/.

Condon, William, Ellen R. Iverson, Cathryn A. Manduca, Carol Rutz, and Gudrun Willett. *Faculty Development and Student Learning: Assessing the Connections*. Indiana UP, 2016.

Dunn, Patricia A. *Learning Re-Abled: The Learning Disability Controversy and Composition Studies*. Heinemann, 1995.

Framework for Success in Postsecondary Writing. Council of Writing Program Administrators, National Council of Teachers of English, and National Writing Project, 2011, wpacouncil.org/framework.

Greenbaum, Andrea. "Nurturing Difference: The Autistic Student in Professional Writing Programs." *The Journal of the Assembly for Expanded Perspectives on Learning*, vol. 16, 2010, pp. 40–47.

Hobgood, Allison P., editor. "Caring From, Caring Through: Pedagogical Responses to Disability." Special Issue of *Pedagogy: Critical Approaches to Teaching Literature, Language, Composition, and Culture*, vol. 15, no. 3, 2015, pp. 413–596.

Huot, Brian, and Peggy O'Neill, editors. *Assessing Writing: A Critical Sourcebook*. NCTE, 2009.

Inoue, Asao, B. *Antiracist Writing Assessment Ecologies: Teaching and Assessing Writing for a Socially Just Future*. Parlor Press and The WAC Clearinghouse, 2015. https://wac.colostate.edu/books/inoue/.

—. "A Grade-Less Writing Course that Focuses on Labor and Assessing." *First-Year Composition: From Theory to Practice*, edited by Deborah Coxwell-Teague, and Ronald F. Lunsford, Parlor Press, 2014, pp. 71–110.

—. "Teaching the Rhetoric of Writing Assessment." *Teaching with Student Texts: Essays toward an Informed Practice*, edited by Joseph Harris, John D Miles, and Charles Paine, Utah State UP, 2010, pp. 46–57.

Kiedaisch, Jean, and Sue Dinitz. "Changing Notions of Difference in the Writing Center: The Possibilities of Universal Design." *The Writing Center Journal*, vol. 27, no. 2, 2007, pp. 39–59.

Lewiecki-Wilson, Cynthia, and Brenda Jo Brueggemann, editors. *Disability and the Teaching of Writing: A Critical Sourcebook*. Bedford/St. Martin's, 2008.

Mackiewicz, Jo, and Isabelle Thompson. *Talk about Writing: The Tutoring Strategies of Experienced Writing Center Tutors*. Routledge, 2015.

MacNeil, Robert. "For Adults with Autism, Few Support Options Past Age 21." *PBS NewsHour Autism Now*, 22 April 2011, www.pbs.org/newshour/bb/health-jan-june11-autism5adults_04-22/.

Mann, April. "Structure and Accommodation: Autism and the Writing Center." *Autism Spectrum Disorders in the College Composition Classroom: Making Writing Instruction More Accessible for All Students*, edited by Val Gerstle and Lynda Walsh, Marquette UP, 2011, pp. 43–74.

Mossman, Mark. "Visible Disability in the College Classroom." *College English*, vol. 64, no. 6, 2002, pp. 645–59.

National Center on Universal Design for Learning. The Center for Applied Special Technology and the U.S. Department of Education, www.udlcenter.org/.

Robertson, Scott M., and Ari D. Ne'eman. "Autistic Acceptance, the College Campus, and Technology: Growth of Neurodiversity in Society and Academia." *Disability Studies Quarterly*, vol. 28, no. 4, 2008, dsq-sds.org/article/view/146/146.

Soliday, M. *Everyday Genres: Writing Assignments across the Disciplines*. SIUP, 2011.

Vidali, Amy. "Disabling Writing Program Administration." *WPA: Writing Program Administration*, vol. 38, no. 2, Spring 2015, pp. 32–55.

—. "Discourses of Disability and Basic Writing." Lewiecki-Wilson and Brueggemann 40–55.

Vidali, Amy, Margaret Price, and Cynthia Lewiecki-Wilson. "Introduction: Disability Studies in the Undergraduate Classroom." *Disability Studies Quarterly*, 28, 4, 2008, http://dsq-sds.org/article/view/137/137. Accessed 7 Feb. 2017.

Walters, Shannon. "Toward an Accessible Pedagogy: Dis/ability, Multimodality, and Universal Design in the Technical Communication Classroom." *Technical Communication Quarterly*, vol. 19, no. 4, 2010, pp. 427–54.

White, Edward M, and Cassie A. Wright. *Assiging, Responding, Evaluating: A Writing Teacher's Guide*. 5th ed., Bedford/St. Martin's, 2015.

White, Edward M., Norbert Elliot, and Irvin Peckham. *Very Like a Whale: The Assessment of Writing Programs*. Utah State UP, 2015.

Wills, Kathy V., and Rich Rice, editors. *ePortfolio Performance Support Systems: Constructing, Presenting, and Assessing Portfolios in Public Workplaces*. The WAC Clearinghouse and Parlor Press, 2013.

Yancey, Kathleen Blake. "Looking Back as We Look Forward: Historicizing Writing Assessment." *College Composition and Communication*, vol. 50, no. 3, Feb. 1999, pp. 483–503.

Yancey, Kathleen Blake, Emily Baker, Scott Gage, Ruth Kistler, Rory Lee, Natalie Syzmanski, Kara Taczak, and Jill Taylor, editors. "Writing Across the Curriculum and Assessment: Activities, Programs, and Insights at the Intersection." Special Issue of *Across the Disciplines*, 3 Dec. 2009, wac.colostate.edu/atd/assessment/.

Steven J. Corbett is Director of the University Writing Center and an assistant professor of English in the Department of Language and Literature at Texas A&M University-Kingsville, a public research university. He is the author of Beyond Dichotomy: Synergizing Writing Center and Classroom Pedagogies, *and co-editor (with Michelle LaFrance and Teagan E. Decker) of* Peer Pressure, Peer Power: Theory and Practice in Peer Review and Response for the Writing Classroom, *and (with Michelle LaFrance) the forthcoming* Student Peer Review and Response: A Critical Sourcebook. *His work in writing studies research and pedagogy has appeared in a variety of academic journals and collections.*

Failures to Accommodate: GTA Preparation as a Site for a Transformative Culture of Access

Casie J. Fedukovich and Tracy Ann Morse

Abstract

This article introduces interview-based data in order to complicate our disciplinary narratives about early-career graduate students as identified primarily by the remediation of their teaching. Instead, we explore the place of disability in the lives of five MA/MFA graduate student teaching assistants (GTAs) teaching first-year writing to argue for more attention to accessibility in teacher preparation programs. We seek to begin conversations about redesigning our physical and pedagogical spaces and practices in service to a "transformative culture of access," defined by its goal of "question[ing] and rethink[ing] the very construct of allow[ance]" (Brewer, Selfe, and Yergeau 153-54). We conclude by arguing for more attention to a flexible, adaptive administrative design for GTA preparation that takes into account principles of universal design to ensure that we strive to address the needs of all GTAs and contingent faculty.

In Fall 2015 at Southeastern State University, only 81 graduate students (across all programs at the university, master's through doctorate) sought accommodations through the Disability Services Office, less than one percent of the 9,904 graduate students enrolled. This number cannot account for the many graduate students who qualify for accommodations but do not seek them.

The process of students self-advocating for accessibility creates a novel challenge when it intersects with the culture and processes of graduate study, including graduate teacher preparation. The First-Year Writing Program at Southeastern State works with approximately 45 master's-level graduate teaching assistants every semester, split between incoming and returning students. The performance-based metrics that we use to evaluate teaching—from in-class mentoring with experienced faculty to classroom observations—can collide with GTAs' unexpressed needs, creating a situation whereby these novice teachers feel both disempowered to ask for help and vulnerable that they need it.

Writing program administrators are tasked with addressing accessibility in first-year writing classes, but no research has explored accessibility for graduate teaching assistants (GTAs) who would benefit from but may not seek accommodations or who may be granted accommodations as students but not as instructors. Likewise, no research has explored the ways in which our GTA teacher preparation practices may be improved for accessibility. In our disciplinary scholarship, GTAs are identified most frequently by their novice teaching status (Bullock); their development as teachers (Dryer; Restaino; Estrem and Reid; Reid, Estrem, and Belcheir); and by their resistance to teacher preparation, including the practicum (Dobrin; Ebest).

Additionally, most extant scholarship contends with doctoral-level GTAs, understandable since these students provide longitudinal data and, the assumption may be, will graduate to join the professoriate.

This article introduces interview-based data in order to complicate our disciplinary narratives about early-career graduate students as identified primarily by the remediation of their teaching. We explore the place of disability in the lives of five MA/MFA graduate student teaching assistants (GTAs) teaching first-year writing to argue for more attention to accessibility in teacher preparation programs. We present these five narratives not to establish any generalizations about GTAs with disabilities. Instead, we seek to begin conversations about redesigning our physical and pedagogical spaces and practices in service to a "transformative culture of access," defined by its goal of "question[ing] and rethink[ing] the very construct of allow[ance]" (Brewer, Selfe, and Yergeau 153–4). To clarify, we argue for writing programs to approach their physical and intellectual spaces of teaching, teacher preparation, and planning in radical ways that encourage user-centered transformations of those spaces.

None of the GTAs in this study advocated for themselves in obvious ways—asking for accommodations, for example—fearful that doing so would make them vulnerable to criticism from colleagues and program administrators. In particular, they worried about how disclosing their disabilities might affect their teaching assistantships, especially since GTAs at Southeastern State teach only in seated, face-to-face (not fully online or hybrid) sections of first-year writing. The culture of graduate school was so pervasively threatening to them that they chose to work off the institutional grid and solve their disability needs themselves, typically without disclosing their struggles to anyone, even peers.

We describe the study before moving to explore the five GTAs' experiences with serving as graduate teaching assistants who self-identify as having a disability. We conclude by proposing a path to taking a disciplinary stance on the role of disability awareness in teacher preparation programs. This piece extends Brewer, Selfe, and Yergeau's call to consider "a culture of access [as] a culture of transformation" (151) while also honoring both accessibility and teacher preparation as complex, iterative social processes (Wood, Dolmage, Price, and Lewiecki-Wilson).

We are compelled as writing program administrators by an ethical obligation to bring attention to the many graduate students in our program who may be laboring as instructors without needed accommodations. As Tara Wood, Jay Dolmage, Margaret Price, and Cynthia Lewiecki-Wilson describe in "Where We Are: Disability and Accessibility," we are looking toward Disability 2.0. Our "what-now moment" finds exigency in the knowledge that we are preparing future teachers without, in many cases, regards for their individual needs. As such, this article aims to "emphasize a dynamic, recursive, and continual approach to inclusion, rather than mere troubleshooting," to describe GTA preparation as a part of our commitment to "an orientation of inclusion" (147–48).

The Study

The data presented here come from a larger study on GTAs' perceptions of threat while in graduate school. In Spring 2015, Casie interviewed eight graduate teaching assistants at Southeastern State, a large, land-grant research university in the southeast.[1] Participants were invited by email. Seven of eight participants completed an introductory survey, an exit survey, and three one-hour interviews. (See Appendix A for survey questions and interview protocol.) One participant completed both surveys and one interview. Half of those interviewed, four of eight, identified diagnosed and treated disabilities, including PTSD, dyslexia, anxiety disorders, ADD/ADHD, and physical disabilities related to chronic pain. One GTA described pervasive anxiety and emotional distress associated with teaching, though she did not seek medical intervention.

The research study emerged from Casie's experience as a writing program administrator tasked with preparing large cohorts of master's-level GTAs to teach first-year writing. The initial study did not explicitly identify disability as a threat faced by graduate students. (See Appendix B for the informed consent approved by the Institutional Review Board.) However, because half of the participants identified as having medically-verifiable disabilities and none sought accommodations, we knew that we had to explore this line of inquiry.

The Participants

Mario is 26 and studies World Literature. His background is in Comparative Literature and Sexuality Studies. His first teaching experience was with his mentor in first-year writing. He described his first year of graduate work as "painful" and "very difficult," culminating in a failed suicide attempt. He described struggling with PTSD and medically treated anxiety, stressors compounded by a number of physical ailments, including mobility issues that caused him to walk with a cane.

Susan is 22, studying rhetoric and composition. She held no prior formal teaching experience, but she described experiences with informal teaching, particularly as a volunteer teacher for students with special needs, where she helped with reading interventions. Susan described herself as "not a very good writer" since she struggles with dyslexia. Her dyslexia causes her anxiety as both a novice teacher and a graduate student. She related that she always struggles with telling her professors about her disability because she's afraid it could "come across as an excuse." Though she has far more professional development than others in her cohort—service with a national journal, attendance at national disciplinary conferences—she feels like she must work "extra hard to make up for [the] potential errors" caused by dyslexia.

Michaela is 35 and studying British and American literature. She entered the program after leaving a career in law, which she described as "stressful, punishing, and too competitive." She had no prior teaching experience, formal or informal, but she indicated that she was excited to get into the classroom. She described a history of struggling with ADHD and ADD and was concerned with the reality of teaching 100-minute classes. "I'm such a people pleaser," she said, "and desperate to do what I'm supposed to do . . . but it's like I have to work three times as hard as everyone else."

Jane is 26 and pursuing her MFA. She identified no prior teaching experience, but she did list leading a creative writing workshop under informal teaching experiences. From her description, she acted as a *de facto* teacher of record. Jane did not disclose a formal medical diagnosis, but she did describe a history of abuse that affects her teaching preparation to the extent that she has sought counseling.

Chloe is 22, also working towards an MFA, and tutored for one year at her BA-granting university. On her entrance survey, she disclosed a diagnosis of PTSD, rooted in a history of physical, psychological, and emotional abuse. Her teaching philosophy is grounded in her experiences with abuse, as she identified one of her goals as helping students who are struggling with hidden (not visible) disabilities. She described graduate school as the "perfect storm" for exacerbating her existing struggles with anxiety: "I think there's a kind of air where you have to act like you're smart and you have everything under control, and you don't. You're judged at every turn, and it can be difficult. The evaluation part can be difficult, and some people are not very nice. And that can be difficult."

Before entering their own classrooms as instructors of record, all five GTAs completed Southeastern State's rigorous teacher preparation program. This program includes shadowing an experienced faculty mentor for one semester, completing two graduate courses—one in composition theory and a teaching practicum—and completing an intensive one-week pedagogy workshop. At the time of interviews, each GTA had taught, as the instructor of record, one section of first-year writing in Fall 2014 and had started their second semester teaching one section of first-year writing in Spring 2015. At Southeastern State, first-year writing is a one-course, four-credit-hour requirement, and each GTA taught seated (not online or hybrid) sections either four days a week for 50 minutes a class or two days a week for 100 minutes a class. In their first semester teaching, Fall 2014, each GTA also attended the pass/fail teaching practicum one day a week.

"It Felt Very Threatening to Me": Teaching as a Dangerous Activity

"Do you think it would be okay if I used my cane in class while teaching?" Mario asked Casie this question as he began preparations to teach his first section of first-year writing in Fall 2014. Of course, Casie advised him to use whatever accommodations he needed to feel comfortable while teaching. In the spring, during formal interviews, Mario went on to narrate some of his fears about teaching, particularly that students would identify his use of a cane as frailty. Though it never emerged in practicum discussions in the fall, in interviews, Mario described situations where students would litter classroom pathways with their bookbags and other personal items. He told Casie, "It didn't feel intentional at all, but I do think that students chose to overlook my cane . . . [In the spring], I came in on the first day and said, 'Sometimes I will have to use this, please get used to it.'" He was concerned, he said, with making a "spectacle" of his disability. Mario identified his age as contributing to his hesitance with using his cane in front of his students: "I'm only 26, so it's not like I can say it's old age. My students will know it's because of something else."

Mario was the only participant to disclose a physical disability, but like two of the other four GTAs, he also identified as having emotional disorders, specifically anxiety and depression, related to the traumatic car accident that led to his mobility issues. Mario's relationship with his faculty teaching mentor was tumultuous, but neither mentor nor GTA contacted Casie to mediate the situation. In Mario's end-of-term teaching evaluation, Mario's mentor formally reported that Mario might struggle with teaching, primarily because his anxiety left him, at times, unfocused and unprepared. Mario came to Casie visibly upset, concerned that the program would choose to terminate his assistantship, a decision held in reserve for only those GTAs who cannot be confidently placed in the classroom.

Mario's stressful situation with his mentor culminated in him attempting suicide during the spring pedagogy workshops. He told Casie that he had not confided in any of his peers or professors, saying,

> The day I was late [for the workshops], something had happened. It was a suicide attempt. It's something I don't like to unload on people because I know it's difficult to deal with. It wasn't anything grand, but it was an ideation that resulted in action . . . because I was so overwhelmed.

He assured Casie, as the WPA who oversees GTA preparation,

> This isn't a reflection on you, but I didn't know what [my mentor] had told you about how I was working out. I don't blame anyone. I would never say to someone, "You drove me to suicide," but the psychological—it was amped up after talking with [my mentor about my teaching].

Mario had thought his mentor had intended to recommend nonrenewal, which would terminate his funding and end his graduate career.

Mario's experience illustrates the need for our research: he struggled with both physical and emotional disabilities, and the teacher preparation process at Southeastern State exacerbated these challenges. He was caught between his graduate student identity, one which acknowledges vulnerability, and his developing teacher identity, where it is assumed he will be focused and prepared at all times. Casie has pondered the many junctures where this situation could have been better addressed: perhaps with increased communication with his mentor along the way, or if Mario had been offered the opportunity to teach online, negating the need for physical presence in a brick-and-mortar classroom. Mario's admission of his suicide attempt stands as a stark example of what can happen when GTAs' needs outside teaching preparation aren't fully considered.

Chloe and Jane likewise narrated complex experiences with anxiety, depression, and teaching. Chloe described growing up in an extremely conservative, religious household as an experience in dislocation, as in her words, "being stuck" in a bad situation and feeling out of place. She described her experience like "growing up in a cult," where women were considered subservient and groomed for marriage and motherhood, not higher education. Chloe's sister committed suicide at age 11. Chloe witnessed the event and still struggles with PTSD. She sees a therapist once a month to "talk through her stress" and gain perspective on the anxiety that attends graduate study. "The program has been supportive," Chloe assured, "People are not terribly critical, but it is still stressful." She used the same term, "shell-shocked," to describe both the aftereffects of her sister's suicide and her acclimation to graduate school. Though Chloe is completing an MFA, her goal is to work in the medical field. Medical school, she admitted, will add to her stress, but graduate school so far has "taught me how to balance [my work and life]," so "I won't be shell-shocked when I get there." Because of her history with PTSD, Chloe identified a pedagogy influenced by invisible challenges. She described a process of teaching that foregrounded student affective need instead of course policies or the like, primarily because she said she "knows how it feels when professors see their own plans for teaching the course as more important than students' desire to learn."

Jane likewise described a history with abuse that influences her relationships with students: "A lot of [my interaction with students] comes from growing up in an abusive household and being the oldest child of three, being the person who was put in charge of managing and protecting other people." These early childhood experiences were followed by an abusive romantic relationship that proved difficult to leave. However, she said these relationships gave her a grounding perspective: "I've been through a lot worse with less, and I can get through [graduate school]. [When I am down,] I am able to turn myself up, and that's very helpful." It is important to note that Jane did not self-identify as having a medically-verifiable disability; however, her anxiety affected how she perceived her role as the teacher on record, and she chose to foreground these experiences with abuse as foundational to her development as a teacher.

During her first year in graduate study, Jane experienced some scary and expensive health issues. She described a few weeks where she thought she would lose her apartment because she couldn't afford rent. During this time, she visited the on-campus food pantry for groceries and found piecework to supplement her income. Jane identifies her difficult past and struggles with anxiety related to abuse as giving her both the strength and determination to push through: "I care about my life, and I want it to look like what I want it to look like. I don't want other people to have power over that."

Jane also expressed that she had experienced unwanted advances from male students, which triggered some of her anxiety about interactions with men. Jane described her pedagogies as "very decentered, the typical writing workshop circle where the teacher wants to hear from everyone." These practices were thrown into question after a tense exchange with a male student during a class discussion, where the student described Jane as "sexy" and "distracting." As a creative writer, she held the power of the open writing workshop as sacrosanct, "but there are those natural moments where me as a small woman who has grown up in her life being intimidated and abused by men, those moments I don't feel safe in the situation." Jane was forced to rethink her pedagogies, concluding that she needed to clearly and calmly express how inappropriate these comments were for the benefit of the entire class and even if it shut down discussion for that day. Being authoritative, she determined, did not run counter to her desire to decenter her classroom; instead, it helped her manage the classroom environment for everyone's comfort and safety. Jane concluded one interview by stating that she knows that some students will transgress boundaries but that it is her responsibility as the teacher on record to maintain them.

Mario disclosed both emotional and physical disabilities; Jane and Chole disclosed emotional disabilities and challenges, specifically PTSD and anxiety. Michaela and Susan, in contrast, disclosed learning disabilities. These disabilities—ADD/ADHD in Michaela's case and dyslexia in Susan's—affected the novice teachers' sense of security and confidence in graduate school and during their teacher preparation. Michaela mentored in a 100-minute section of first-year writing, an experience that forced her to consider her own learning needs within the frame of her developing pedagogies: "I have ADD, and I would have trouble getting back on track [in class]," she said of her experience as student. As a novice teacher, she worked with her faculty mentor to plan ways of supporting her teaching needs while also supporting students' learning needs. As the teacher of record, Michaela said that she disclosed her disorder to her students to build community and encourage those who need accommodations to ask for them. Michaela's experiences with ADD and ADHD also encouraged her to rethink what engagement looks like in her classroom, and she framed her teaching with students with learning disabilities in mind. For example, she would diversify the classroom modalities, incorporating written and aural instruction, kinesthetic learning, and collaborative learning. She was aware of environmental features like noise and light and their potential effects on students.

During her first semester as instructor of record, one student, Michaela said, "self-identified as having ADHD, and he said he realized that taking the 100-minute class was not the best choice for him. We talked about how he might consider taking shorter classes." Michaela could recognize her own struggles in this student's experience, and she honored his effort, saying, "[I can see] he's trying, he's fighting." Our interviews were the first time Michaela had mentioned her struggle with ADD and ADHD. She was placed in a 100-minute section for her mentoring semester and then in a 100-minute section for her first teaching semester. She had requested 50-minute classes in the fall, but indicated that 100-minute sections would be acceptable but not preferred. Because of the many intricacies in scheduling over 90 sections of first-year writing a semester, we ask all faculty to give us a range of available teaching times. Our scheduling process tends to value seniority first, with long-time faculty granted their first choices. Graduate students, because they teach only one section and have the least seniority, are generally considered last and typically in the context of their coursework schedules over their preferences. As a result, we unintentionally placed Michaela in a teaching situation that exacerbated her disability.

Like Michaela, Susan disclosed a history with a learning disability, specifically dyslexia. She described her graduate school experience thus far as rewarding but challenging, since she felt as if she had to work doubly hard to produce (and, with teaching, assess) written products. "I'm dyslexic," she said, "and I have a really hard time with grammar and mechanics and that can be paralyzing in a lot of ways." Her dyslexia was co-morbid with anxiety and bi-polar disorder, a "sort of perfect storm," she said, when it came to the challenges of graduate study. Living away from home for the first time amplified her experiences, as she noted, "I was really nervous living by myself in this very unfamiliar place. The first thing I had to do when I got here was find a doctor." After acclimating to her new living arrangements and schedule, Susan said that she could better focus on her coursework and preparation to teach. Writing for evaluation "can be a difficult thing for [her] to do," and she admitted that she has a

> hard time taking criticism for [her] writing because it's so much easier to believe the bad stuff because of how I think of myself as a writer. I'm not very good at absorbing the good things when I write because I'm so focused on the ways I could improve.

This anxiety with sharing her work with her graduate-school peers influences the way she conducts her own classroom, as she always worked to alleviate anxiety for all of her students. Susan never identified the practicum as an uncomfortable space, however students are required to conduct peer teaching observations and to peer review a number of course documents, including their evolving teaching philosophies. Though the modality for peer reviews was left open to individual pairs, so students could review paper copies or use a digital sharing service like Google Docs, each student was required to participate as a part of the course. With the new knowledge of Susan's dyslexia and the anxiety it creates with peer review, Casie began to rethink this element of the teaching practicum.

"THANKFUL FOR THE PERSPECTIVE": LESSONS FROM GTAs

Sibylle Gruber reminds us that GTAs often feel like "[t]here is nothing we can do about it" in regards to their low status in the program and their felt needs (35–37). As with teaching, those responsible for teacher preparation cannot possibly account for every need of every student in class. As a number of critics of Universal Design point out (Dolmage "Disability Studies Pedagogy"; Vidali; Yergeau et al.), the idea that we can ever design a classroom, or a preparation process, for all students overstates the flexibility of even the most flexible designs. In "Mapping Composition: Inviting Disability in the Front Door," Jay Dolmage reminds us that "UD is not tailoring of the environment to marginal groups; it is a form of hope, a manner of trying" (24). A single best-practice approach to GTA preparation is not successful; there is not a universally designed teacher preparation program we can pick up and use from place to place or with group to group. What we have learned from the GTAs in this study is that we can use principles of Universal Design to help us engage in a process that transforms our preparation of and support for GTAs. These principles extend to our administrative work with all faculty teaching in our writing programs, and particularly contingent faculty who may not feel empowered to self-advocate. After all, "Universal Design is a process, a means rather than an end" (Yergeau et al.) The framework of Universal Design often neglects continued feedback from users, but if we reinforce Universal Design as a process, we can create spaces and practices where all individuals have a part in recreating those spaces and practices (Dolmage "Disability Studies Pedagogy").

These GTAs, much like the students in our first-year writing classes, are adept at navigating difficult situations, often without our assistance. They can pass without us as administrators noticing the barriers we have constructed in our preparation practices (see Brueggemann's "On (Almost) Passing" for more on the complexities of identity often experienced by academics with disabilities). We may think in terms of accommodations, especially those familiar to us as teachers of students with disabilities. While being aware of accommodations may be a step in the right direction, in practice it is a problematic framework to use. Yergeau et al. explain that "accommodations are usually discussed in terms of individuals' needs; thus, they tend to locate a disabled individual as a problem, even when this is not the intention" (n.p.). To extend this thought further, it is our approach to teacher preparation and supporting GTAs that has identified participants by the visible and invisible barriers we have constructed. We can learn from their perspectives and argue for a recursive preparation practice that is flexibly designed. Our GTAs are not problems to be solved, nor is our accepted language on accommodation the solution.

All five participants identified a sort of self-reliance that came out of their histories with disabilities and a desire to push through the rigors of graduate study, even—and especially—when their coursework or teaching duties exacerbated their struggle. What we have learned from these GTAs, and others, is that the work of passing can become the detrimental main focus with wide ranging results:

> When I get to feeling this way—trapped, nailed, stuck in between overwhelming options—I tend to become frantic, nervously energized, even mean. And my will to pass, to get through and beyond at all costs, kicks in ferociously. Some animals freeze in fear, shut down in fright; I run–harder, faster, longer. I run until I pass—until I pass on, or out. (Brueggemann "On (Almost) Passing" 655)

While Brueggemann is focusing on her own experiences feeling displaced in Deaf and Hearing cultures, the participants in this study faced their own emotions when it came to passing or disclosing their disabilities to the students they taught. The GTAs faced this decision during a time in their careers when they are also balancing the rigors of graduate-level expectations.

To counter this exacerbation, WPAs can transform the culture of their writing programs and GTA preparation structure to become a culture of access. What is necessary in this transformation is the clarity of the participants that they are indeed participants—they should be encouraged to provide feedback, to be co-creators of the culture of access. We need to promote the "*disabling* of writing program work" that Amy Vidali argues for in "Disabling Writing Program Administration" (33; emphasis original). Doing so, we will make our work accessible and inclusive, authentically including "how disability can inform all writing program work by drawing attention to the bodies that do such work" (Vidali 33). WPAs must create a culture that affords all participants in that program invited perspectives to constantly recreate the culture.

Transforming GTA Preparation, Troubling Accommodations

Disability scholarship in first-year writing has focused primarily on the ways teachers might be more responsive to student need and, more recently and pertinent to this study, the intersection of contingency and disability. The preliminary findings presented here not only implicate new discussions in teacher preparation; they also, because many of these GTAs will become our non-tenured colleagues, force us to continue to consider the role of disability in the lives of those who are insecurely employed. This discussion necessarily implicates discussions of contingency and calls for increased attention to how instructors off the tenure track navigate disability.

Sushil K. Oswal reminds us in "Ableism" that the Americans with Disabilities Act (ADA) promises to remove barriers for people with disabilities. We often see the work of the ADA in retrofits—ramps, Braille signage, sign language interpreters. Oswal points out that the work of the ADA at institutions of higher education is nominal at best:

> exclusionary practices at various institutional and interpersonal levels continue to flourish even at colleges where significant resources have been invested in developing disability-related administrative policies and guides. How often do faculty using wheelchairs need to remind their colleagues that a meeting in a less distant part of the campus would enable them to participate without losing precious time maneuvering through circuitous paths and barely accessible buildings? How many times do visually impaired faculty members have to hear that the presenter forgot to email them the handouts in advance, but that they will make sure to email them as soon as possible? How often does it occur to the presenter that a disabled faculty member cannot fully participate in the meeting without the resources everyone else can readily access in real time? (n.p.)

The dependence of many of our WPA peers and colleagues on the ADA to do the work of creating access for all program participants is not enough. We argue that WPA work needs to be interdependent (much like the participatory design and interdependence that comes from an ethical infrastructure that Margaret Price argues for in "Space"). The GTAs we train and support in their early teaching should be encouraged as contingent faculty to participate in the collaborative work of a writing program. Their participation should impact the culture of access of that program.

We know that what we are calling for is a significant change to ways of thinking and ways of administering. We know that WPAs are often overworked and underappreciated, and many may respond to this call for transformation with "Oh, no, not one more thing." However, it is from the role of the WPA where change can emerge. We are not arguing for WPAs to anticipate individualized solutions for specific types of disabilities. We want WPAs to be flexible and adaptable in the intellectual and physical spaces they engage in with faculty (all instructors—GTAs, contingent, tenure-track, tenured). We must also state that we are not arguing for WPAs to become therapists. We want WPAs to use more inclusive language that purposefully does not exclude faculty with physical or psychiatric disabilities. What message might we send when we refer to something being lame or insane? In "Community," Elizabeth Brewer points to the invaluable support peer-run communities are providing psychiatrically disabled people. We may want to borrow from this discussion the framework of "safer spaces" Price explains in *Mad at School*:

> Safer *kairotic* spaces could take many forms, including gatherings of friends, sessions of private writing, or—as is suggested by Jane Thierfeld-Brown, who works with students with Asperger's syndrome—'safe rooms' on her college's campus for students to visit if they need a break from the constant stimulation of more public space. (100)

If WPAs encouraged safer spaces among their faculty and GTAs, then a transformation of the culture moves to more accessibility and inclusivity.

WPAs need to acknowledge the discriminatory, at worst, and problematic, at best, GTA preparation practices that have held court for so long and, instead, encourage a transformation for a culture of access. By being transparent about expectations and flexible and adaptive to ways of meeting expectations, by encouraging participatory reciprocity, and by using inclusive language, we may pick up momentum for significant change that will better address the needs of *all* GTAs and contingent faculty.

NOTES

1. This study was granted IRB clearance by the NC State IRB board, Protocol Number 5213. All names and places (except NC State) are coded.

APPENDIX A: DATA COLLECTION PROTOCOL

TA recruitment email
Dear TAs:

I am writing to invite you to participate in a research project I am conducting.

This project is tentatively titled "Perceptions of Threat: GTAs and Material, Psychological, and Physical Harm." The purpose of this study is to explore the many different kinds of threats that GTAs encounter during their time in graduate school, from intellectual threats from peers and professors to the looming threat of what comes next and the potential threats accompanying teaching for the first time. By gathering individual narratives, I hope to be able to better address GTAs' needs in the future.

Participants' narratives will be kept confidential, and all identifying features will be coded. Participants may also elect to drop out of the study at any point without consequence.

I will be scheduling private introductory meetings between 1 November and 30 November. At this meeting, I will review our research process and answer any questions you might have. Please reply to me at cjfeduko@sesu.edu or stop by my office at XXXX if you are interested in learning more about the project or if you would like to attend an introductory meeting. Attendance at this meeting does not assume that you will participate in the study.

Participation in this study is strictly voluntary and not participating will have no influence on your standing in the First-Year Writing Program or the English Department. Participation is limited between November 2014 and May 2015, and includes surveys, three one-hour interviews, and one optional focus group.

As always, you can stop by my office (XXXX) or email with questions.

Best,
Casie

Text for introductory survey (Dec. 2014)

Perceptions of Threat: GTAs and Material, Psychological, and Physical Harm
Introductory Survey
Participant Copy

Name:

Coded name (please choose a pseudonym to use throughout the study):

Age:

Cohort membership: 1ˢᵗ year   2ⁿᵈ year

Area of study:

Prior degrees awarded:

Years teaching before participation in this project. (Teaching is here defined as acting as the instructor of record in a formalized educational environment: K12, higher ed., etc.):

Do you have additional informal teaching experience that may inform your participation in this project (tutoring, leading discussion groups, etc.)? Briefly describe these experiences and their duration:

Use the remainder of this space to include any additional information you feel is pertinent to your participation in this study:

Protocol for first individual interview (Jan. 2015)

What made you interested in participating in this project?

Tell me a little about your decision making process when it comes to continuing into graduate study. What, if any, options did you consider before making your decision?

Can you describe for me a little bit about your experience in graduate school so far? What have been some of the most rewarding aspects? What about the most challenging?

Protocol for second individual interviews (Feb. 2015)

For these spring discussions, we're going to use a process that the business world calls a SWOT matrix—an exploration of the complex interaction of strengths, weaknesses, opportunities, and threats.

For today's interview, we're going to use the following diagram to talk about the SWOT protocol in two areas: your identity as a graduate student and your performance/identity as a teacher or soon-to-be teacher.

First, what would you describe as your strengths in graduate study, as a student?

Your weaknesses?

Your opportunities?

Your threats?

What would you describe as your strengths as a teacher/soon-to-be teacher?

Your weaknesses?

Your opportunities?

Your threats?

External Influences

	Opportunities	Threats
Strengths	How do you leverage your strengths to benefit from opportunities?	How do you use your strengths to mitigate threats?
Weaknesses	How do you ensure your weaknesses will not stop you from opportunities?	How do you address your weaknesses to mitigate threats?

Internal Responses

Protocol for third individual interviews (April 2015)

For this final interview, we're going revisit the SWOT protocol, using it to talk about your plans for what comes next, after you graduate. Describe your plans after graduation, even if they're tenuous or nebulous. Then we'll fit these plans in the SWOT matrix, using the prompts below:

External Influences

	Opportunities	Threats
Strengths	How do you leverage your strengths to benefit from opportunities?	How do you use your strengths to mitigate threats?
Weaknesses	How do you ensure your weaknesses will not stop you from opportunities?	How do you address your weaknesses to mitigate threats?

Internal Responses

Text for Exit Survey (May 2015)

Coded name:

Cohort membership: 1st year 2nd year

Briefly define the word "threat," in the context of your professional experiences:
Rate the following areas on a scale of 1 to 5, with 5 being "most confident"
and 1 being "least confident."

My performance as a student in a graduate classroom

1 2 3 4 5

What experiences have led you to assign your student performance
this ranking?

My performance as a teacher of record

1 2 3 4 5

What experiences have led you to assign your teacher performance this ranking?
Given that the focus of this study is on perceptions of threat, what topics
do you feel are most relevant to address with graduate teaching assistants?
Why these topics?

Protocol for *optional* Focus Group (May 2015)

Describe one day, in composite, that you feel is illustrative of your
spring semester.

APPENDIX B: INFORMED CONSENT SOUTHEASTERN STATE UNIVERSITY

INFORMED CONSENT FORM for RESEARCH

Perceptions of Threat: GTAs and Material, Psychological, and Physical Harm

Dr. Casie Fedukovich, Principle Investigator

What are some general things you should know about research studies?

You are being asked to take part in a research study. Your participation
in this study is voluntary. You have the right to be a part of this study, to
choose not to participate, or to stop participating at any time without penalty. The purpose of research studies is to gain a better understanding of a
certain topic or issue. You are not guaranteed any personal benefits from
being in a study. Research studies also may pose risks to those that participate. In this consent form you will find specific details about the research
in which you are being asked to participate. If you do not understand some-

thing in this form it is your right to ask the researcher for clarification or more information. A copy of this consent form will be provided to you. If at any time you have questions about your participation, do not hesitate to contact the researcher(s) named above.

What is the purpose of this study?

This study seeks to explore the types of "threats"—physical, psychological, intellectual, and emotional—Graduate Teaching Assistants (GTAs) in the First-Year Writing Program (FYWP) at SE State may perceive as they enter the classrooms for the first time. As novice teachers and scholars, GTAs find themselves immersed in a range of new and emotional experiences, from teaching to participation in high-pressure graduate courses and considerations of future employability. Extant research on graduate students looks at their identity negotiations (Restaino) and their relationships to students as writers (Dryer). As Jessica Restaino points out, much that has been written about graduate TA training focuses on how these students effectively assimilate the mores of academia and their home program. No studies have yet looked at the constellation of perceived threats GTAs may experience, which the PI argues is an important factor for keying GTA training to unspoken needs. This study in which you are invited to participate is important because it extends this line of inquiry to look at the constellations of anxieties particular to this population in the hopes of improving graduate TA training by accounting for perceived threats.

What will happen if you take part in the study?

Participation is limited between November 2014 and May 2015. This research process includes attendance at three individual interviews in Spring 2015; attendance at one optional focus group in Spring 2015; and completion of two surveys (an introductory survey and an exit survey). between January 2015 and May 2015; approximately 1 hour of mixed-methods data completion, including the two surveys (introductory and exit).

If you agree to participate in this study, you will be asked to complete the following steps, in chronological order:

1 Nov.–30 Nov. 2014: Attend a private meeting to review IRB, Informed Consent, and the research process. Meetings will be held in XXXX 232, a private faculty office.

Dec. 2014: Complete the introductory survey.

Jan. 2015: Attend first individual interview, held in XXXX 232.

Feb. 2015: Attend second individual interview, held in XXXX 232.

April: 2015: Attend third individual interview, held in XXXX 232.

On or around **1 May 2015**: Attend *optional* focus group and complete exit survey.

Risks

There are two notable risks associated with participation in this study. First, the PI also serves as your direct teaching supervisor. Participation may create undue stress on this relationship. Participation is strictly voluntary, and you may stop participating at any time. Your participation will not affect your teaching review or your potential consideration for teaching award nominations or other opportunities. If you feel that you have experienced unfair judgment in these areas as a result of your participation in this project, you may contact the Director of First-Year Writing, [removed name], at XXX-XXX-XXXX.

Second, participation in this study may elicit discussions about specific kinds of threats, which may trigger past traumas or create anxiety. The PI will not ask direct questions about specific past threats. All discussions of these experiences will be participant driven. You will receive all individual and focus group interview questions in advance and may notify the PI if you feel uncomfortable discussing any question or if you feel that discussion would negatively impact your standing in the program. In the event that you do wish to seek additional psychological or psychiatric support, you may visit SE State Counseling Center at XXX XXXX Avenue. You may reach the Counseling Center by phone at XXX-XXX-XXXX or on the web at http://. . . /counseling-center/.

Benefits

There is no direct benefit to your participation in this project. However, by better understanding the range and types of threats GTAs experience, we can better adjust our graduate student training to account for these threats and thus provide more grounded and better contextualized preparation.

Confidentiality

The information in the study records will be kept confidential to the full extent allowed by law. Data will be stored securely in a locked faculty office, with digital records kept password protected. No reference will be made in oral or written reports which could link you to the study. All names and other identifying materials will be coded.

Compensation

You will not receive anything for participating.

What if you are a SESU student?

Participation in this study is not a course requirement and your participation or lack thereof, will not affect your class standing or grades at SE State.

What if you are a SESU employee?

Participation in this study is not a requirement of your employment as a GTA at SE, and your participation or lack thereof, will not affect your job.

What if you have questions about this study?

If you have questions at any time about the study or the procedures, you may contact the researcher, Casie Fedukovich at XXX-XXX-XXXX (cell), by email at cjfeduko@sesu.edu, or on campus in XXXX 232._

What if you have questions about your rights as a research participant?

If you feel you have not been treated according to the descriptions in this form, or your rights as a participant in research have been violated during the course of this project, you may contact XXXX).

Consent to Participate

I have read and understand the above information. I have received a copy of this form. I agree to participate in this study with the understanding that I may choose not to participate or to stop participating at any time without penalty or loss of benefits to which I am otherwise entitled.

Subject's signature_____ Date _____

Investigator's signature_____ Date _____

WORKS CITED

Brewer, Elizabeth. "Community." In "Multimodality in Motion: Disability and Kairotic Spaces." *Kairos*, vol. 18, no. 1.

Brewer, Elizabeth, Cynthia L. Selfe, and Melanie Yergeau. "Creating a Culture of Access in Composition Studies." *Composition Studies*, vol. 42, no. 2, 2014, pp. 151–54.

Brueggemann. Brenda Jo. "On (Almost) Passing." *College English*, vol. 59, no. 6, Oct. 1997, pp. 647–60.

Bullock, Richard. "In Pursuit of Competence: Preparing New Graduate Teaching Assistants for the Classroom." *Administrative Problem Solving for Writing Pro-*

grams and Writing Centers: Scenarios in Effective Program Management. Edited by Linda Myers-Breslin, pp. 3–13. NCTE, 1999.

Dobrin, Sidney. Don't Call it That: The Composition Practicum. NCTE, 2005.

Dolmage, Jay. "Disability Studies Pedagogy, Usability, and Universal Design." Disability Studies Quarterly, vol. 25, no. 4, Fall 2005.

—. "Mapping Composition: Inviting Disability in the Front Door." Disability and the Teaching of Writing: A Critical Sourcebook. Edited by Cynthia Lewiecki-Wilson and Brenda Jo Brueggemann. Bedford/St. Martin's, 2008.

Dryer, Dylan. "At a Mirror, Darkly: The Imagined Undergraduates of Ten Novice Composition Instructors." College Composition and Communication, vol. 63, no. 3, 2012, pp. 420–52.

Ebest, Sally Barr. Changing the Way we Teach: Writing and Resistance in the Training of Teaching Assistants. SIUP, 2005.

Estrem, Heidi, and E. Shelley Reid. "Writing Pedagogy Education: Instructor Development in Composition Studies." Exploring Composition Studies: Sites, Issues, and Perspectives. Edited by Kelly Ritter and Paul Kei Matsuda, pp. 223–39. Utah State UP.

Gruber, Sibylle. "When Theory and Practice Collide: Becoming a Feminist Practitioner." Performing Feminism and Administration in Rhetoric and Composition Studies. Edited by Krista Ratcliffe and Rebecca Rickley, pp. 31–52. Hampton Press, 2010.

Reid, E. Shelley, Heidi Estrem, and Marcia Belcheir. "The Effects of Writing Pedagogy Education on Graduate Teaching Assistants' Approaches to Composition." WPA: Writing Program Administration, vol. 36, no. 1, 2012, pp. 32–73.

Oswal, Sushil K. "Ableism." In "Multimodality in Motion: Disability and Kairotic Spaces." Kairos, vol. 18, no. 1.

Price, Margaret. Mad at School: Rhetorics of Mental Disability and Academic Life. U of Michigan P, 2014. kairos.technorhetoric.net/18.1/coverweb/yergeau-et-al/pages/space/index.html

—. "Space." In "Multimodality in Motion: Disability and Kairotic Spaces." Kairos, vol. 18, no. 1.

Restaino, Jessica. First Semester: Graduate Students, Teaching Writing, and the Challenge of Middle Ground. NCTE/SIUP: 2012.

Vidali, Amy. "Disabling Writing Program Administration." WPA: Writing Program Administration, vol. 38, no. 2, Spring 2015, pp. 32–55.

Wood, Tara, Jay Dolmage, Margaret Price, and Cynthia Lewiecki-Wilson. "Where We Are: Disability and Accessibility," Composition Studies, vol. 42, no. 2, 2014, pp. 147–50.

Yergeau, Melanie, Elizabeth Brewer, Stephanie Kerschbaum, Sushil K. Oswal, Margaret Price, Cynthia L. Selfe, Michael J. Salvo, and Franny Howes. "Multimodality in Motion: Disability and Kairotic Spaces." Kairos, vol. 18, no. 1. kairos.technorhetoric.net/18.1/coverweb/yergeau-et-al/pages/space/index.html

Casie J. Fedukovich is an assistant professor in English and Associate Director of the First-Year Writing Program at North Carolina State University, a four-year public research university. Her research interests focus on writing program administration, teaching assistant preparation, and labor issues in composition. Her work has appeared in WPA: Writing Program Administration, FORUM: Issues about Part-Time and Contingent Faculty, *and* Composition Studies, *among other journals. As Associate Director of the First-Year Writing Program, she teaches the GTA teaching practicum and graduate composition history seminar.*

Tracy Ann Morse is Director of Writing Foundations and an associate professor of rhetoric and composition in the Department of English at East Carolina University, a four-year doctoral granting university. Her research and writing are in the areas of disability studies, deaf studies, and composition studies. Her work has been published in Rhetoric Review, Disability Studies Quarterly, Inventio, *and* Journal of Teaching Writing. *Her book,* Signs and Wonders: Religious Rhetoric and the Preservation of Sign Language, *was published by Gallaudet University Press. In addition, she co-edited* Reclaiming Accountability: Using the Work of Re/Accreditation to Improve Writing Programs *and* Critical Conversations about Plagiarism.

Saying No to the Checklist: Shifting from an Ideology of Normalcy to an Ideology of Inclusion in Online Writing Instruction

Sushil K. Oswal and Lisa Meloncon

ABSTRACT

Writing Studies finds itself looking to outside sources in an attempt to understand disability, differing abilities, and accessibility. As a result, in an effort to make our online courses accessible, we often turned to as varied sources as Universal Design for Learning (UDL), Quality Matters Rubric (QM), and Web Content Accessibility Guidelines (WCAG), which we are referring to as checklists, due to their form and instrumental purposes. Programmatically and administratively, we seem to have accepted checklists at face value as something we simply need to adopt and/or implement rather than something to question. With the growing number of students with disabilities in our online classrooms, we argue that such reliance on checklists perpetuates an ideology of normalcy, and we ask, instead, that we start WPA work from the location of disability and accessibility. When we do so, we encourage direct participation from our disabled students and faculty in our theory, in our research, in our curricular planning, and in our pedagogical conceptualizations. Starting with access helps us move toward an ideology of inclusion.

Writing Studies has produced a significant body of scholarship that takes a critical and engaging stance on key issues in the field. However, the critical momentum of this scholarship loses all of its force in some crucial settings, such as online writing instruction (OWI). It seems the field makes an almost a 90-degree turn in which research is discarded in favor of checklists at key pedagogical moments. Rather than rolling up our sleeves and face the task using the field's own scholarly acumen, the field too readily looks for crutches designed by any self-styled outside expert. Of late, disability and accessibility and their implementation in online writing courses (OWCs) have been such a topic.

Over the past decade a growing group of Writing Studies scholars have produced a sizeable body of critical scholarship around issues of disability and accessibility (e.g., Dolmage, *Disability*; Kerschbaum; Lewiecki-Wilson and Brueggemann; Meloncon, *Rhetorical*; Oswal, "Participatory"; Slatin and Rush; Walters; Zdenek). However, this scholarship has failed to adequately address the programmatic and pedagogical issues associated with moving OWCs online. Writing studies finds itself fumbling for answers in trying to understand disability, differing abilities, and accessibility, and as a result, we often turned to outside sources such as Universal Design for Learning (UDL), Quality Matters Rubric (QM), and Web Content Accessibility Guidelines (WCAG), to name the most common. Whereas borrowing and adapting from other fields is nothing new for Writing Studies, our immediate discontent with these checklists is the failure to adequately engage with them in a critical way (Dolmage; Oswal, "Physical"; Wood et al.). We are using checklist as a catchall term to mean a heuristic that provides a list of actions that should be taken to make OWCs accessible. In general, the checklist provides suggestions for implementation of the most basic levels of accessibility. Programmatically and administratively, we seem to have accepted checklists at face value as something we simply need to adopt and/or implement rather than something to question.

In what follows, we take up this question of wholesale adoption of accessibility checklists in OWI, and we do so because accessibility affects a college population—estimated at eleven percent of undergraduates and eight percent of graduates (US Dept. of Education)—that has been historically ignored or underserved by our universities. By building on the existing scholarship specific to OWI and accessibility (see Hewett and DePew; Oswal and Hewett; Oswal and Meloncon; CCCC OWI committee), we first situate our argument theoretically within the related work provided by scholars in Writing Studies and Disability Studies. In the next section, we discuss the most commonly used approaches to online course design, the Quality Matters assessment rubric (QM), Web Consortium Accessibility Guidelines (WCAG), and the Universal Design for Learning framework (UDL). In the last section, we propose participatory approaches as an essential step in realizing the goal of a user-centered accessible design for OWI that will enable fully inclusive and accessible classrooms.

A CRITICAL EXPLICATION OF OWI DESIGN APPROACHES

With at least a third of all students taking a course online (Allen and Seaman), the need to ensure that our online writing courses are accessible to students with disabilities becomes a paramount concern. Further, with many students not identifying as disabled when they enter college (Roberts et al; Schelly, et al; Wagner et al), instructors face additional challenges of trying to determine how to meet the needs of students with disabilities. The importance of designing accessible online learning spaces was clearly highlighted with the publication of the Conference on College Communication and Composition's Position Statement of Principles and Example Effective Practices for Online Writing Instruction. Principle 1, which is described as an overarching principle, states: "Online writing instruction should be universally inclusive and accessible." To help achieve this goal and to assist faculty who may have little understanding about accessibility standards from both a curricular, technical, and legal standpoint, many institutions are adopting standards that are produced by outside organizations and often include the implementation of a checklist.

While checklists are meant to help facilitate inclusive and accessible classrooms (both online and face-to-face) by providing faculty a starting place on issues where they may not have a lot of experience, unfortunately they are often both the starting and ending place for accessible course design. As Sushil Oswal and Lisa Meloncon reported, many faculty are not "paying attention" to accessibility, and they do not realize that part of their role as instructors is to play a major role in making their OWCs accessible. To do so means they have to move beyond the simplistic approach offered by checklists because in many ways checklists are simply another way of enforcing the "ideology of normalcy" (Moeller and Jung).

Moeller and Jung discuss the ways that existing beliefs about OWI are helping to reinscribe the ongoing problem of both students and online education as being "less-than substitutes for the 'real' versions," and then they offer an important theoretical perspective when they "[attend] to the ways in which the dynamics of online education . . . reinscribe an ideology of normalcy." As WPAs and institutions are struggling to provide sufficient professional development for faculty to create OWCs, more often than not they turn to checklists to provide guidance to faculty caught in unfamiliar territory often with few institutional resources to help guide them. The checklists are one way that program administrators and faculty are being encouraged to normalize their classrooms. Online writing courses, then, become sites that potentially restrict access to those students who are outside of the realms of normal, particularly when most checklist-based OWCs would not meet most accessibility standards; that is, OWCs that only follow a checklist will most often not meet the needs of the majority of students with disabilities. Thus, the ideology of normalcy is continued.

Our critical attention has to turn to OWI because instructors have a responsibility to conceptualize an accessible course design, to create its content that reflects the differences of its users, and to select or make allowances for its technology choices that embrace these users' abilities and skill-levels. This approach to OWC design must also apply to the learning management system and extend to third-party content, such as audio and video elements, library materials (e.g., e-books and .pdf articles) and external web pages, which must offer the same level of access to disabled students as it provides for others. Thus, course design, content, and technology should enable all students instead of erecting barriers for students with disabilities. Beyond the accessibility of content in an OWC, instructor-student and student-to-student interaction requires special attention because not all disabled students want to fit into the mold of ableist, or normal, interactions and many might benefit from alternative means of sharing, exchanging, and transferring ideas, information, texts.

To create truly accessible courses means that it becomes necessary to move beyond thinking in terms of checklists. To situate our discussion further, in the next section, we look at the three most common checklists: Quality Matters, Web Content Accessibility Guidelines, and Universal Design for Learning. All of these are used to plan, implement, and assess online course construction and delivery.

Quality Matters (QM)

QM is a national benchmark for online course design that is centered on peer review (by instructors who have been QM certified) using rubrics.

Currently in its fifth edition, the QM rubric workbook includes a section on accessibility and usability, but due to copyright restrictions that limit reproduction to subscribed institutions only, all the components cannot be listed here. However, the overarching problem with the QM rubric is that the advice is still painfully general and limited, and if integrated, would not necessarily meet even basic standards of accessibility. The first criteria (that one can find with an Internet search) is that "course navigation facilitates ease of use." This is a general guideline that can be found in any number of checklists and in a multitude of resources about moving courses online. What Writing Studies can learn from user experience design and usability is that while this seems to be a straightforward and useful criterion, this is much easier said than done. For example, Mahli Mechenbier brought attention to the fact that many institutions have mandated the use of templates in their content/learning management systems, and those templates often do not receive the type of usability tests necessary to determine whether the mandated course navigation actually facilitates ease of use for students, much less students with disabilities. Likewise, Patrick Lowenthal and Charles Hodges applied the QM checklist in their evaluation of six MOOCs, but their results acquired through this rubric failed to bring up any information about the accessibility of these online courses for disabled students. Furthermore, it is extremely telling that QM has added a specific disclaimer to their website about the accessibility criteria of their own guidelines: "Meeting QM's accessibility Standards does not guarantee or imply that specific country/federal/state/local accessibility regulations are met. Please consult with an accessibility specialist to ensure that accessibility regulations are met" (www.qualitymatters.org/rubric). This disclaimer helps to situate the limitations of the QM accessibility component while placing disability in an exclusionary category, particularly when many faculty who may be reviewing courses to certify them may not be fully versed in the wide variety of disabilities students may face. Questions that need to be critically considered include: How might a QM reviewer address all the accessibility barriers for all the students in the design phase? How does an instructor navigate through decision-making process for the choice of delivery tools without a context-specific understanding of technology, particularly when our courses are social media-rich and the learning environments are highly interactive?

Web Content Accessibility Guidelines (WCAG) 2.0

The World Wide Web Consortium established WCAG guidelines in their second edition, and they offer an acronym-based checklist, POUR, for creating accessible web content (www.w3.org/TR/UNDERSTANDING-WCAG20/intro.html). Since OWCs are delivered online, WCAG guidelines have applicability both for content creation and delivery of content. POUR equates to perceivable, operable, understandable, and robust, and WCAG provides a series of examples and guidance instructions for implementation. However, the failure of widespread adoption of WCAG guidelines within OWI may be because they seem too technical. They have been primarily designed to support software developers and may seem targeted to an industry perspectives that reflect the user needs based on detailed, long-term empirical studies and participatory design research. While these guidelines are relevant for developing web-based LMS to ensure technical access to screen reader and keyboard users, and even could be of use to faculty developing their own course websites, these guidelines lack the context-specific knowledge-base that instructors of online courses can build through the experience of working with disabled students over time. For example, researchers like Christopher Power et al., who have studied the usability of these guidelines, report that WCAG 2.0 address only about half of the problems that blind users face in typical web pages.

Questions about these guidelines that need to be critically considered include: How well can guidelines designed for software industry concerns serve the needs of online learners and educators? How does the technical focus of these guidelines detract us from the pedagogical needs of our disabled students? And most crucially, should the living experience architecture of our teaching and learning environments be guided by the machine-centric ethos of WCAG?

Universal Design for Learning (UDL)

Likewise, the principles of Universal Design (UD) have been adopted without critical attention to its usefulness for OWI work. These principles were originally conceptualized for architectural design (Mace) and later adopted by CAST as Universal Design for Learning (UDL) for K–12 curriculum in face-to-face settings. The curriculum designers behind the development of UDL Guidelines, Anne Meyer and David Rose, originally described UDL as a framework but now call them a tool in their CAST promotional materials. The UDL principles stress that instructors provide learners with Multiple Means of Representation, Action and Expression, and engagement. Beginning with the Rehabilitation Act of 1973, and under incrementally improved Individuals with Disabilities Education Act of 1977 (more commonly known as IDEA), schools were legally obligated to include disabled students in all the educational programs. The Special Education teachers, who had quite a range of disabled students with differing needs and abilities at their hand, had an urgent need for a formulaic accessibility structure that would lend to adapting their existing curricula for this diverse cohort. At the same time, these Special Education and other subject matter teachers did not want to engage in the actual pedagogy of access and did not have any other reliable resources to learn access from bottom up. UDL became a straightforward rubric to work with for the school curriculum specialists and to provide Special Education teachers with a ready-made curriculum that could pass as accessible for all at the state and national level.

UDL was never intended as a stand-in for critical engagement with accessibility issues for curricula planning, particularly in online environments. As far back as in 2002, composition scholars Patricia Dunn and

Kathleen Dunn de Murs presented simple remedies to improve accessibility in OWCs based on UDL. While their work raised awareness about the need for accessible academic spaces, the current conception of UDL is a far cry from re-imagining whole pedagogies as Dunn and Dunn de Murs expected. Outside the United States, particularly in Europe, the UD terminology also has been criticized for its universalist claims. The seven UD principles themselves also have been critiqued for moving design activity away from producing objects and environments to the authoring of abstract codes and standards, and despite its user-centered claims, it has been blamed for turning people into abstractions (Sandhu). We also want to highlight that even though UDL's stated goal is to build inclusive course design from bottom up, its design process focuses on checklists—the policy aspect—rather than on the individuals and learners. It can easily verge into another formulaic approach like QM when the implementers of the UDL guidelines lack a meaningful understanding of disability and are not already well-versed in accessible pedagogy. The questions that need to be critically considered include: How can instructors without sufficient knowledge about disabilities and disabled learners can come up with appropriate means of representation, action and expression, and engagement? How can WPAs simply insert an existing curricular framework of the kind of UDL into our online writing instruction training without engaging our faculty in some serious preparation for learning about disability, accessibility, and accessible technologies?

The most basic critique to checklists as a means to create OWCs is that they propose a one size fits all model—a re-inscription of normalcy—because they present course design as something that simply needs to be checked off. This is a model WPAs and faculty need to critically question. We might also stress the obvious that every human being is different and so are the disabilities, some due to the varied psycho-physical differences among bodies and others arising out of the restrictive socio-physical environments surrounding these selves. Consequently, the one size fits all QM, WCAG's POUR method, and UDL is hard to adapt for human processes that involve information processing, imagination, critical thinking, and a whole array of mental and physical processes embedded in the acts of conceptualizing, composing, and designing on and off-line writing. While recent scholarship provides more specific suggestions on making courses accessible (e.g., Oswal and Meloncon; Oswal "Accessibility" and "Physical"), WPAs and faculty need to start pushing back against the checklist mentality because the fact is that many institutions and instructors assume that following these heuristics makes their course(s) accessible, which is not necessarily true.

Thus, there is certain irony found in Tara Wood et al.'s response to the question "whether there is a checklist of things that writing teachers can do to make their classrooms more accessible"; however, they respond with a mixed "yes and no." Wood et al. assert that that checklists are useful as far as they "offer a place to start", but they also emphasize that the checklist can make the process reductive (147). Using any checklist without critical engagement and awareness of strategies to address multiple types of disabilities from our perspective only means that courses will have the patina of accessibility without true engagement and implementation. Our brief analysis of these checklist-based guidelines is aimed at providing administrators and faculty insights into how they should use these tools with a pinch of salt and rather take the next constructive step toward participatory design to become critically engaged in the serious work of building organic accessibility in their programs while making a good-faith effort at accepting disability at par with all other constituencies.

Emphasizing the dynamic nature of all learning interactions, as well as recognizing the diverse needs and capabilities of students with disabilities like other learners, we propose the adoption of participatory design approaches as ongoing processes that program administrators and instructors should regard as central to constructing, implementing, and modeling access in OWI programs and OWCs. What we are arguing for is a move from an ideology of normalcy to an ideology of inclusion. An ideology of inclusion recognizes the experiences and understandings of disabled participants—both as students and instructors—so that a crucial reconfiguring can occur within pedagogies and programmatic structures to move curricular design beyond ableist notions represented by checklists and rubrics. Inclusion in such an ideological formation is a way of seeing, doing, and being, and it must be integrated into curricular design and pedagogical practices, which will be the only way exclusionary legacies of ableism are replaced by participatory values of equity, agency, and inclusion.

Participatory Design Approaches for Moving beyond Checklists

Amy Vidali asks, "how we can revise our WPA narratives to better include disability and diverse embodiment?" (34). To this we would add "how can we revise these narratives in a way that moves us past the ideology of normalcy?" One way to do this is to consider other methods for designing inclusive classrooms that pay attention to disability and diverse embodiments. One such approach is participatory design, which most simply defined is an approach to design where all stakeholders play an active role in the development of a product, service, or information to ensure that all users' needs are met.

Bonnie Nardi reminds us that "today's complicated, interactive systems should not be researched, designed, or tested in laboratories in isolation from the actual users; they demand a participatory process at all stages of design, development, and deployment." Participatory design has long been a successful approach in workplace practice and has been studied and discussed in technical and professional communication (e.g., Balzhiser et al; Oswal; Salvo; Read, et al). Moreover, some scholarship that looks at or incorporates UD and/or UDL is also focusing on participatory design, which could be a potential way to critically move beyond checklists and make OWI truly inclusive and accessible. Allen Brizee, Morgan Sousa, and Dana Driscoll provide a link between universal design and participatory design. Brizee et al. build on their previous work and discuss the usability research that went into the re-design of Purdue University's Online Writing Lab, particularly how they collaborated with other programs on campus to assist students with disabilities. Their work is a specific example in how collaboration across units and attention to participatory design can work toward creating learning services that are inclusive for all students.

Patricia McAlexander and Danielle Nielsen both advocate for using versions of universal design in ways that move beyond the checklist or heuristic approach, and their pedagogical practices are more in line with the principles and practices of participatory design. For example, McAlexander calls for shifting pedagogies to incorporate the whole class into decision-making about learning methods and common topics. Nielsen, too, incorporates participatory design into her curricular practices, such as her decision to provide multiple assignment choices for students to achieve specific learning outcomes. While neither McAlexander nor Nielsen frame their pedagogical choices in the language of participatory design and neither move beyond a cursory examination of UDL, both provide important examples that could be implemented in OWC design.

For OWI, participatory design can accomplish a number of important goals:

- Give students a voice in curriculum design.
- Ensure students with disabilities can access course material.
- Provide a forum for all students—not just those with disabilities—to voice suggestions or concerns about course content.
- Enable increased buy-in in the course curriculum and/or program.
- Balance student voice with learning outcomes.
- Encourage student-centered and experiential pedagogies.

Some examples of specific activities where instructors can easily implement participatory design include

- Create multiple assignments where students can choose.
- Use mid-term evaluations to evaluate not only course content but accessibility features.
- Implement end-of-term focus groups with students as part of professional development activities for faculty.
- Create a community of practice for your program to share accessibility features that have been successful for OWCs (see Meloncon and Arduser for details).
- Work with the instructional designers or those in charge of templates for the LMS to test those templates with students, including students with disabilities (see Brizee et al.).
- Take up self-study projects with potential research value for acquiring first-hand knowledge of accessibility barriers our students face by learning adaptive technology, such as, a screen reader or a voice recognition program, and using it for testing your campus learning management system tools (see Oswal, "Accessible")

In OWI work so far, instructional designers, scholars, and instructors have not engaged disabled participants systematically even though participatory approaches encourage collaboration with disabled students to arrive at well-tested course design and delivery models. It might be important to point out that each disabled user participates in online technologies and pedagogies from an entirely different vantage point shaped by their social, physical, and educational experiences. Similarly, each user interacts with multimodality differently depending upon the body they got, the adaptive technology they employ on their end, and the uses they have for multimodality in their repertoire of learning tools.

Consequently, only ongoing participatory studies can build a reliable knowledge base for designing OWI. By this time, readers would have realized that accessibility problems do not exist simply because of lingering issues from the pre-ADA era, random technological gaps, or missing pieces of furniture in the classroom—although these also contribute significant accessibility barriers. These problems are far more deeply rooted in the exclusionary institutional structures—structures without visible bodies that have a stranglehold over the machinery of systemic change in the form of university, departmental, or academic policies we have developed over time. What we're arguing for is that participatory design has to become a central component of OWI production technologically, pedagogically, and culturally in order to exert pressure for change in institutional policies and structures.

Our purpose of employing participatory design methods is to launch longitudinal studies conceptualized for building continuous feedback loops. Participants could not only be partners in original course design stages but also have the capacity of constantly analyzing their interactions with an online course platform, while simultaneously assessing the usability and accessibility of various tools, content, and pedagogical techniques. Examples of immediate areas where participatory design could be engaged is in content storage (downloading and uploading documents); machine delivery (access to the asynchronous content being staged such as traditional and streaming videos, information present on web pages, etc.); and interaction tools (discussion boards, chat spaces, collaboration wikis, quiz building and hosting platforms, etc.). This sort of collaborative course construction would provide ongoing feedback specific to how an OWC actually performs when it is operationalized as a living course.

IMPLICATIONS OF PARTICIPATORY DESIGN FOR WRITING PROGRAM ADMINISTRATION

Participatory accessible design is entrepreneurial, has the potential of becoming an ultimate arbiter for usability, and can advance innovative pedagogical methods. While proponents of user-centered design (e.g., Albers and Mazur; Redish and Barnum; Norman 1988) have advocated for practical, useful, and customer-focused designs, their definition of customer/user has remained selective, designer-centered, and focused on a typical able-bodied user (Meloncon "Technological"). We would like to emphasize that those in human-centered design, such as designers and developers, continue to view users from an ableistic lens, and their involvement in participatory design remains mostly restricted to the able-bodied, and after-the-fact fixes or retrofits to accommodate disabled users' needs are the norm than an accidental exception. Even when the needs of this group receive attention, rather than integrating the affordances of accessibility theory into our baseline design theory and practice, those in human-centered design relegate such work to a separate corner, thus pushing accessibility and disability even farther in the margins. We emphasize that this process of implementing the participatory design of programs, courses, and assignments should not be limited to certain categories of disabilities. Even when in our teaching approaches we try to integrate disabled students as constituents and stakeholders, our specific pedagogical strategies stop short of being inclusive of the gamut of disabilities represented among our students.

From the perspective of student-centered learning approaches, the affordances of participatory design offer an altogether unexplored field of educational opportunities both for scholarly research and teaching innovation where program administrators, instructional designers, and faculty in charge of putting together the curriculum and delivering it as online writing courses, have the chance of coming face-to-face with online disabled students as active agents and learn from them about their ways of interacting with our pedagogy.

From the perspective of faculty engagement, participatory responses to faculty training for accessible design and delivery of online curriculum supplies a unique opportunity to place faculty with disabilities in key positions as participants, leaders, co-trainers, and shapers of academic programs while assisting the institution integrate disabled students and disability in every aspect of the university life. Participatory design approaches offer an incentive for deans and chairs to become proactive rather than reactive to the growing threat of legal suits for noncompliance with disability laws.

From an administration perspective, these approaches can provide valuable data that can be used to advance curricular changes as well as to argue for resources for faculty development opportunities. Ongoing participatory feedback about accessibility issues from disabled students in each of our courses and the resulting iterative design and pedagogical improvements by faculty and instructional designers not only can ensure that programs are legally and ethically compliant with existing laws and regulations but also elevate the overall quality of our programs. Our movement to participatory design invokes the scholarly voices of Moeller and Jung who called for more research with actual students. Their perspective, as well as ours, advocate for research studies in OWI that would provide important data for making administrative cases on improving OWCs.

Within this broader argument for participatory approaches is the more nuanced argument that students with disabilities are not monoliths who can be cordoned off into one campus corner with Disability Services and their accessibility concerns cannot be addressed with a checklist. What we want to underscore is that the solutions offered by easy-to-apply checklists can make instructors and programs deceptively feel good about having paid attention to accessibility even when these lists are most likely not making our courses or our programs accessible in any meaningful manner.

We are pointing to specific participatory design approaches to get beyond these checklists so that root-level attitudinal and institutional shifts could become possible through ongoing re-visioning and reimagining of institutional spaces and policies for removal of barriers through the direct involvement of the primary stakeholders. We intend these participatory approaches as a collaborative teaching and learning project among disabled and non-disabled faculty, students, and staff. These participants can also assist institutions of higher education in speeding up the process of making third-party software and systems accessible through continuing reporting of design issues and functional glitches with learning tools and content management systems. We need not spell out that we are suggesting a whole new way of employing participatory design methods to build accessibility capacity in writing programs while engaging our faculty, disabled, and non-disabled students in undergraduate research. Scholars and teachers conducting participant design research can further employ methodological tools such as rapid ethnography, expert consultation, user diaries, observation 'in situ', and testing with prototypes, tools popularized by design industry to give voice to student ideas who are at the forefront as learners but can also enable user-facilitated innovation.

CONCLUSION

We previously argued that the field had to begin to build capacities in writing programs by training graduate students and faculty in issues of accessibility: "for accessibility to be effectively implemented across programs requires a fundamental shift in ideology; it requires starting with accessibility as a parallel to learning outcomes" (294). Moving away from checklists, which promote an ideology of normalcy, and toward participatory curriculum design affords programs a way to think of OWC design in terms of an ideology of inclusion.

Our effort in this article has been to share the ways of thinking about access as a participatory, scholarly project for our programs than prescribing another set of course characteristics as a checklist for building access. We have chosen this path to advancing access in OWI not only because students with disabilities are diverse and require differing pedagogies but also because the institutions of higher education and instructors are also equally diverse. While this diversity does not give us an excuse to ignore or marginalize our disabled students, it endows us with differing opportunities and abilities to think about how we have so far approached the questions of access without input from almost every fifth of our students and how we could redesign our programs and curricula with this type of participatory studies—ones that are fulfilling for all our students in achieving their learner goals and equally satisfying for us as researchers and teachers.

Even though external standards of access—whether they relate to the content of our web pages (WCAG 2.0) or to the concept and structure of our pedagogy (UDL 2.0)—might give us an implementable and universally useable framework for designing access for our students, an ultimate move towards a more inclusive access depends on how we perceive ourselves and our students. Tobin Siebers once asked,

> What difference to human rights would it make if we were to treat fragility, vulnerability, and disability as central to the human condition, if we were to see disability as a positive, critical concept useful to define the shared need among all people for the protection of human rights?

Looking at the frailties of our own bodies more closely when defining ability and disability, and more importantly access, allows Writing Studies an opportunity to enter into truly collaborative partnerships between administrators, instructors, and students to make our programs and pedagogies more inclusive. We would argue that it is only appropriate that all bodies— labeled as disabled or non-disabled—take an active role in this institutional work by participating as co-designers in university structures, policies, programs, and curricula. We need to start our WPA work from disability and accessibility. When we do so, we encourage direct participation from our disabled students and faculty in our theory, in our research, in our curricular planning, and in our pedagogical conceptualizations. Starting with access helps to create an ideology of inclusion.

Works Cited

Albers, Michael J., and Mary Beth Mazur. *Content and Complexity: Information Design in Technical Communication*. Lawrence Erlbaum Associates, 2003.

Allen, I. Elaine and Jeff Seaman. "Grade Change: Tracking Online Education in the United States." 2014. Babson Survey Research Group and Quahog Research Group.

Balzhiser, Deborah, Paul Sawyer, J. Smith, and Shen Womack. "Participatory Design Research for Curriculum Development of Graduate Programs for Workplace Professionals." *Programmatic Perspectives*, vol. 7, no. 2, 2015, pp. 153–172.

Brizee, Allen, Morgan Sousa, and Dana Driscoll. "Writing Centers and Students with Disabilities: The User-Centered Approach, Participatory Design, and Empirical Research as Collaborative Methodologies." *Computers and Composition*, vol. 29, no. 4, 2012, pp. 341–66.

CAST. *Universal Design for Learning Guidelines* 2.0 edition, CAST, 2011.

CCCC Committee for Best Practices in Online Writing Instruction. "A Position Statement of Principles and Example Effective Practices for Online Writing Instruction (OWI)." NCTE, 2013. www.ncte.org/cccc/resources/positions/owiprincipleshttp://www.ncte.org/cccc/resources/positions/owiprinciples.

Dolmage, Jay. "Disability, Usability, Universal Design." *Rhetorically Rethinking Usability*, edited by Susan Miller-Cochran and Rochelle Rodrigo, Hampton Press, 2009, pp. 167–90.

—. *Disability Rhetoric.* Syracuse UP, 2014.

Dunn, Patricia A., and Kathleen Dunn De Mers. "Reversing Notions of Disability and Accommodation: Embracing Universal Design in Writing Pedagogy and Web Space." *Kairos*, vol. 7, no. 1, 2002,

Hewett, Beth L., and Kevin DePew. *Foundational Principles of Online Writing Instruction.* The WAC Clearinghouse and Parlor Press, 2015.

Kerschbaum, Stephanie. *Toward a New Rhetoric of Difference.* NCTE, 2015.

Lewiecki-Wilson, Cynthia, and Brenda Jo Brueggemann. *Disability and the Teaching of Writing: A Critical Sourcebook.* Bedford-St. Martin's, 2008.

Lowenthal, Patrick R., and Charles Hodges. "In Search of Quality: Using Quality Matters to Analyze the Quality of Massive, Open, Online Courses (MOOCs)." *The International Review of Research in Open and Distributed Learning*, vol. 16, no. 5, 2015, n.p.

Mace, Ron. "The Principles of Universal Design, Version 2.0." North Carolina State www.design.ncsu.edu/cud/ about_ud/udprinciples.html.

McAlexander, Patricia. "Using Principles of Universal Design in College Composition Courses." *Curriculum Transformation and Disability: Implementing Universal Design in Higher Education*, edited by Jeanne L. Hugbee, Center for Research on Developmental Education and Urban Literacy, General College, University of Minnesota, 2003, pp. 105–14.

Mechenbier, Mahli. "Putting the 'Temp' in Template: Molding Contingent Faculty into Uniform Online Course Shells." *Conference on College Composition and Communication* NCTE, 2015.

Meloncon, Lisa. *Rhetorical AccessAbility: At the Intersection of Technical Communication and Disability Studies.* Baywood, 2013.

—. "Technological Embodiments." *Rhetorical AccessAbility: At the Intersection of Technical Communication and Disability Studies*, edited by L. Meloncon, Baywood, 2013, pp. 67–81.

Meloncon, Lisa, and Lora Arduser. "Communities of Practice Approach: A New Model for Online Course Development and Sustainability." *Online Education 2.0: Evolving, Adapting, and Reinventing Online Technical Communication*, edited by Kelli Cargile Cook and Keith Grant-Davie, Baywood, 2013, pp. 73–90.

Moeller, Marie and Julie Jung. "Sites of Normalcy: Understanding Online Education as Aprosthetic Technology." *Disability Studies Quarterly*, vol. 34, no. 4, 2014, n.p.

Nardi, Bonnie A. "The Use of Ethnographic Methods in Design and Evaluation." *Handbook of Human-Computer Interaction*, edited by M.G. Helander and P. V. Landauer, vol. 1, Elsevier Science, 1997, pp. 361–66.

Nielsen, Danielle. "Universal Design in First-Year Composition: Why Do We Need It? How Can We Do It?" *The CEA Forum*, vol. 42, no. 2, 2013, pp. 3–29.

Norman, Donald A. *The Design of Everyday Things.* Doubleday, 1988/2002.

Oswal, Sushil. "Accessible Eportfolios for Visually-Impaired Users: Interfaces, Designs, and Infrastructures." *Eportfolio Performance Support Systems: Constructing, Presenting, and Assessing Portfolios.* edited by Katherine Willis and Rich Rice, Parlor Press, 2013.

—. "Commentary: Participatory Design: Barriers and Possibilities." *Communication Design Quarterly*, vol. 2, no. 3, 2014, pp. 14–19.

—. "Physical and Learning Disabilities in OWI." *Foundational Practices of Online Writing Instruction*, edited by Beth L. Hewett and Kevin DePew, The WAC Clearinghouse and Parlor Press, 2015, pp. 253–90.

Oswal, Sushil, and Beth L. Hewett. "Accessibility Challenges for Visually Impaired Students and Their Online Writing Instructors." *Rhetorical AccessAbility: At the Intersection of Technical Communication and Disability Studies*, edited by Lisa Meloncon, Baywood, 2013, pp. 135–56.

Oswal, Sushil, and Lisa Meloncon. "Paying Attention to Accessibility When Designing Online Courses in Technical and Professional Communication." *Journal of Business and Technical Communication*, vol. 28, no. 3, 2014, pp. 271–300.

Power, Christopher, André Freire, Helen Petrie, and David Swallow. "Guidelines Are Only Half of the Story: Accessibility Problems Encountered by Blind Users on the Web." *SIGCHI Conference on Human Factors in Computing Systems CHI '12. ACM*, ACM, 2012, pp. 433–42.

Read, Sarah, Anna DelaMerced, and Mark Zachry. "Participatory Design in the Development of a Web-Based Technology for Visualizing Writing Activity as Knowledge Work." *SIGDOC '12 Proceedings of the 30th ACM International Conference on Design of Communication*, ACM, 2012, pp. 333–40.

Redish, Janice (Ginny), and Carol Barnum. "Overlap, Influence, Intertwining: The Interplay of UX and Technical Communication" *Journal of Usability Studies*, vol. 6, no. 3, 2011, pp. 90–101.

Roberts, Jodi B, Laura A. Crittenden, and Jason C. Crittenden. "Students with Disabilities and Online Learning: A Cross-Institutional Study of Perceived Satisfaction with Accessibility Compliances and Services." *Internet and Higher Education*, vol. 14, no. 4, 2011, pp. 242–50.

Salvo, Michael. "Accessible Information Architecture: Participatory Curricular Design." *Annual Conference of the Council for Programs in Technical and Scientific Communication*, Council for Programs in Technical and Scientific Communication, 2003.

Sandhu, Jim. "The Rhinoceros Syndrome: A Contrarian View of Universal Design." *Universal Design Handbook*, edited by Wolfgang Preiser and Korydon Smith, vol. Second, McGraw-Hill, 2011, pp. 44.43–44.11.

Schelly, Catherine L., Patricia L. Davies, and Craig L. Spooner. "Student Perceptions of Faculty Implementation of Universal Design for Learning." *Journal of Postsecondary Education and Disability*, vol. 24, no. 1, 2011, pp. 17–30.

Siebers, Tobin. "Disability and the Right to Have Rights." *Disability Studies Quarterly*, vol. 27, no. 1/2, 2007, http://dsq-sds.org/article/view/13/13.

Slatin, John M. and S. Rush. *Maximum Accessibility*. Addison-Wesley, 2003.

US Department of Education, National Center for Education Statistics. "The 2012 Statistical Abstract, Table 285. Students Reported Disability Status by Selected Characteristics 2007 to 2008." 2012. US Department of Education.

Vidali, Amy. "Disabling Writing Program Administration." *WPA: Writing Program Administration*, vol. 38, no. 2, 2015, pp. 32–55.

Wagner, Mary, Lynn Newman, Renee Cameto, Nicolle Garza, and Phyllis Levine. *After High School: A First Look at the Postschool Experience of Youth with Disabilities*. SRI International, 2005.

Walters, Shannon. *Rhetorical Touch: Disability, Identification, Haptics*. U of South Carolina P, 2014.

Wood, Tara, Jay Dolmage, Margaret Price, and Cynthia Lewiecki-Wilson. "Moving Beyond Disability 2.0 in Composition Studies." *Composition Studies*, vol. 42, no. 2, 2014, pp. 147–50.

World Wide Web Consortium. "Understanding WCAG 2.0." World Wide Web Consortium.

Zdenek, Sean. *Reading Sounds: Closed-Captioned Media and Popular Culture*. U of Chicago P, 2015.

Sushil K. Oswal is an associate professor of Accessible Design and technical communication at the University of Washington, a four-year public research university. He specializes in human-centered design and disability studies. His award-winning research has appeared in Kairos, *the* Journal of Business and Technical Communication, Communication Design Quarterly, *and several edited collections.*

Lisa Meloncon is an associate professor of technical and professional communication in the Department of English at University of South Florida, a four-year public research university. She specializes in rhetoric of health and medicine, disability studies, and programmatic issues in technical and professional communication. Her award-winning research has appeared in journals such as Technical Communication Quarterly, Technical Communication, *and the* Journal of Business and Technical Communication. *She is also the editor of* Rhetorical Accessibility: At the Intersection of Technical Communication and Disability Studies.

Kindness in the Writing Classroom: Accommodations for All Students

Kelly A. Shea

ABSTRACT

In this essay, I remind readers that the composition classroom can be an apt model for how active learning should take place and that, as WPAs and writing teachers, we should consider interdisciplinary approaches that promote inclusivity for differently abled—and all—students. Perhaps it doesn't matter what abilities students have, as long as everyone is treated fairly, receives assignments that are built for success, is given extra time when requested, and is allowed to use a computer, for example. This benefits everyone and singles out no one. So why not accommodate all of our students in these ways? This essay examines inclusive pedagogical approaches in the context of several students' composition experiences—to what extent have active learning, universal design, or simply patient, thoughtful teaching affected their experiences in writing classrooms? Can't we just teach all students in a more friendly and humane way? I believe we can—and should.

A September, 2015, article in *The New York Times* "Sunday Review" addressed the notion of whether the college lecture format was unfair. The writer, Annie Murphy Paul, showed that some students who sit in lecture-based versus active learning classes are discriminated against and thus perform less well than other students (Paul). She pointed out that "minority, low-income, and first-generation students face a[nother] barrier in traditional lecture courses: a high-pressure atmosphere that may discourage them from volunteering to answer questions, or impair their performance if they are called on" (Paul).

Paul might just as well have been describing the experiences of students with physical, learning, or emotional disabilities; they are often similarly silenced. The good news for writing program administrators, faculty, and

WPA: Writing Program Administration, vol. 40, no. 3, 2017, pp. 78–93.

78

students is that the typical writing classroom is the perfect model for how active learning can and should take place; this is learning and teaching that can benefit all students, and, in particular, those with so-called disabilities. In fact, when writing about the difficulties of being inclusive across the many types of college classes and classrooms that exist, Rick Godden and Anne-Marie Womack acknowledge that "it is not lost on us that our experiences with small writing-intensive classes are markedly different than those of instructors with hundreds of students in lecture halls" (n. pag.). The good news for most composition teachers is that we do teach in settings that allow for paying more close attention to each student. Thus, on a daily basis, we as writing teachers and administrators would rather do well by our students by considering what interdisciplinary approaches to teaching writing promote inclusivity, for differently abled—and, indeed, all—students. Being inclusive, for example, means creating assignments that give everyone a chance to succeed. Does it matter what abilities students have or don't have, as long as everyone is treated fairly, is given extra time when requested, and is allowed, perhaps, to use a computer? These practices benefit everyone and single out no one. So why not accommodate all of our students in these ways? As Jay Dolmage points out in his book *Disability and the Teaching of Writing*, can we plan for diversity in the classroom rather than react to it (21)? Can't we just teach all of our students in a more friendly and humane way?

Undertaken herein is an examination of inclusive writing-pedagogy approaches that would benefit all students as well as discussion of several students' academic experiences with and/or opinions of this idea. To what extent have active learning, universal design (Roberts et al. 5), or simply patient, thoughtful teaching affected their experiences or their perceptions of others' experiences? What if accommodations were offered to everyone? What would happen?

It was Paul's article as well as recent discussions about college writing with a new friend that brought these pedagogical matters to the forefront. I met a young woman, Donna, in my exercise class.[1] As I got to know her, I learned that she was in her early '30s and had taken dozens of classes at two local community colleges over a period of several years in an attempt to earn her associate's degree. She explained that she had multiple learning and anxiety issues, and she had trouble focusing and participating in the classroom, taking notes, reading effectively, and writing coherently, among other challenges. She had spent her high school and college careers struggling, being called stupid, feeling like a failure, and having zero confidence in herself academically and otherwise. Somehow, she had persevered and had gotten almost to the point of achieving her goal of an associate's degree, but one course that stood between her and the degree. Her nemesis was Composition 2. She had taken it 11 times and had dropped it six times and outright failed it five times.

At the same time, we had discussed how our exercise class was helping with some of her focus issues, and at one point, I asked, "Why don't you try Comp 2 again?" So, she did. She ended up in a class with an instructor who was in tune with students with disabilities like Donna's—not to mention that this was a professor who understood how to work with the accommodations that were legally due Donna and others. She passed Comp 2 and got her associate's degree the following spring. Her confidence soared, she started taking additional classes (including math, another nemesis, and even creative writing courses), and she is now considering enrolling in the local four-year college (not where I work) to pursue her bachelor's degree. Her struggles with academic work continue, but her experience getting over that seemingly insurmountable hurdle has also increased her self-advocacy and her own attempts to make peace with her so-called disabilities.

Donna's story reminded me of some of the stories of my own students, and I realized that the reasons for these students' successes focused on their persistence and their professors' abilities to support them. It also occurred to me that many of the so-called accommodations that we are asked to provide for our students by our Disability Support Services (DSS) offices and by the students themselves are so simple and straightforward that we might consider whether they—or even some of them—could be afforded to all students, in some ways. In their article, "Making Disability Part of the Conversation: Combatting Inaccessible Spaces and Logics," Godden and Womack suggest that

> there is no *one* answer even within one classroom. In contrast to singular best practices such as a universal ban on screens in classrooms, disability studies promotes multi-modal options and flexible design. When information and tasks are presented across multiple modes, it opens choices for *all* users about how best to access that information (first emphasis in original; second emphasis added).

As it turns out, this broadened form of teaching and learning is not necessarily a new concept—at least not across elementary, secondary, and, somewhat more recently, post-secondary education. Many so-called accommodations for so-called learning disabilities fall under the category of the concepts known as Universal Design for Learning (UDL) or Universal Design for Instruction (UDI), or, simply, Universal Design. While these concepts were developed with learning disabled (or differently abled) students in mind, Danielle Nielsen, in her article on UDL and first-year composition in *The CEA Forum,* points out that "As a praxis . . . UDL attempts to address all students' needs, not just those with disabilities, and suggests that rather than focusing on specific disabilities and interventions, teachers should ensure information is accessible in many different ways" (6).

This concept is borne out in the research in several ways. In their review of studies of UDI in postsecondary educational practice, Roberts, et al., documented a study in which a large-enrollment special education undergraduate course employed, among other theories, UDI principles to

> develop predictable and accessible instruction for individuals with diverse abilities, address their varied learning pace and prerequisite skills, minimize nonessential physical effort, stimulate student interest and attention by presenting information in different mediums [sic], and create a welcoming and inclusive instructional environment. Student evaluations indicated the course was better than other courses offered in the department and other undergraduate courses, including their particular appreciation for making course materials online. (12)

Certainly, this type of success in a large classroom bodes well for college writing classrooms, which, according to the Conference on College Composition and Communication, should be no more than 20 students.

The idea of offering accommodations to all students cuts across several layers in a writing program administrator's work—teacher training, classroom teaching, and student learning. However, my particular interest is not simply in what teachers of writing can/should/might/will do in this regard—we are certainly in charge of our own pedagogy, and much of what we do naturally no doubt follows UD principles, as described below. But what do students involved in such classrooms think of this idea? What would students with diagnosed disabilities think about allowing all students to have accommodations that were designed with differently abled students in mind, especially accommodations that the students might have worked hard to secure for themselves? On the other side of the coin, as it were, how would students without diagnosed disabilities feel about being afforded certain accommodations without being asked? In a student-centered approach to teaching, in which, as described by Stes and Van Petegem in their study of approaches to teaching, there is a "focus on what the students are doing . . . [and where] the teachers . . . help students develop their conceptions . . . or change their conceptions" (645); perhaps it's most appropriate—indeed, it's paramount—to ask the students.

Before getting to the students, though, just what accommodations are we talking about? I have mentioned several above. In his book, *Universal*

Design in Education: Teaching Nontraditional Students, Frank Bowe notes that

> universal design challenges us to think again about who should be responsible for accessibility . . . . Universal design asks us to look at courses, texts, schedules, and other aspects of education: Is it really necessary for teachers to present the great bulk of our instruction via speech? Isn't there a way, or aren't there several ways, for us to offer much of the same material visually . . . ? Of course, the obverse obtains as well: Must we assign only printed materials for student reading? Can't we find audible (spoken) versions, too, and make those available for people who need or prefer them? (2).

Bowe (and others) describe seven (or nine for higher education) principles for Universal Design, which boil down to a few simple ideas:

> present information in multiple ways . . . offer multiple ways for students to interact and respond to curricula and materials . . . provide multiple ways for students to find meaning in the material and thus motivate themselves . . . make good use of . . . course web pages. (4–5)

Further into the twenty-first century, of course, this latter point means accessible course management systems and other digital technologies, but these remain valid principles, as discussed by Roberts, et al. (6–7), in the following list:

PRINCIPLES OF UNIVERSAL DESIGN IN HIGHER EDUCATION

- **Equitable use**: Accessing course information, such as syllabi, in a variety formats, including print, disk, and online.
- **Flexibility in use**: Varying instructional methods, including lecture, discussion, and individual and group activities.
- **Simple and intuitive**: Clearly describing course expectations for grading, in different formats, for example narrative and rubrics.
- **Perceptible information**: Using videos that include subtitles, or captioning, for those who may not hear, for whom English is not a first language, or for those who have trouble processing verbal information.
- **Tolerance for error**: Providing ongoing and continual feedback on coursework rather than at specified interim periods, such as mid-term or final exams.
- **Low physical effort**: Providing lecture notes, so students who have difficulty taking notes do not need to take notes.

- **Size and space for approach and use**: Making seating easily accessible, if possible, so everyone can see each other and communicate with one another directly. Circular seating may address this principle.
- **Community of learners**: Creating a variety of learning settings, for example, use of email groups, social networking sites, or chat rooms.
- **Instructional climate**: Including a statement in the syllabus indicating the desire to meet the instructional needs of all students and for students to convey their needs to the instructor.

Several years later in 2006, again as described by Roberts et al, a study was conducted by McGuire and Scott with focus groups

> to explore the validity of UDI as a new construct . . . Instructional methods described by the student participants that make up a "good" college course included: clear expectations, organizational materials such as course outlines and study guides, information presented in multiple formats (e.g., lecture with visuals), affirmative classroom experiences, associating information with aspects of real life, frequent formative feedback, supportive of diverse learning needs, and effective assessment strategies . . . The authors noted that participant reports regarding attributes of high quality college courses . . . parallel the guiding principles of UDI. (9)

WRITING CLASSROOM UDI-INFLUENCED PEDAGOGIES

It is, perhaps, obvious from the list above how these ideas might work in the writing classroom, but what are some specific suggestions? In a perfect academic world, here's a start:

- Offer all students the option to use a laptop or other typing device in the classroom for informal writing as well as for in-class tests (if the latter is even necessary).
- Offer all students the option to use electronic books and/or online texts of some sort.
- Provide deadline extensions for both in-class and out-of-class writing assignments when requested/possible, or offer blanket extensions.
- Minimize lecture in the classroom and in office hours.
- Offer extended time on essay tests—or any tests.
- Provide written feedback on essay drafts.
- Provide clear/concise/written essay assignment sheets.
- Offer teacher-provided class notes (when relevant).

So, now, finally, to the students. I had informal conversations with six college students (three of whom replied via email and three of whom replied in conversation), with varying degrees of learning disabilities—or no diagnosed learning disabilities—who have recent experience in writing classrooms in high school and college. None of them were my students; in fact, none of them attend my institution. I asked them a series of open-ended questions (Appendix A) about their experiences with and/or observations of accommodations in the writing classroom. Did diagnosed students who were offered writing-related accommodations use them? Were they helpful? Were they (and non-diagnosed students) aware of other students who used accommodations? What benefit (if any) did such students enjoy? What is the opinion of both diagnosed and non-diagnosed students regarding offering all students accommodations in the writing classroom?

Generally speaking, the students seem to have no significant problems with making so-called accommodations available to all students, although a few of the students did take varying levels of issue with the idea. While the logistics of some of these accommodations could be difficult (Donna—the student mentioned above who does receive official accommodations—mentioned that perhaps not every student can get preferential classroom seating or alternate-site testing, for example), the idea of creating academic situations in which students can do better on their writing assignments makes sense to them. As Kevin (a student who does not receive official accommodations) points out, "Students should without exception be offered whatever accommodations are needed to allow them to achieve their maximum individual writing potential."

However, there were student concerns that focus on the ways that non-learning-disabled students might take advantage of some of these accommodations. The most common concern is that, if all students were allowed to have laptops in the classroom, they could take advantage of the opportunity to, for example, look up answers to questions that they should know from the reading that they should have done, or engage in even less productive work, like scrolling their social media sites or engaging in online shopping or checking their fantasy sports teams. This was both Saima's (a student who does not receive accommodations) and Georgie's (a student who did receive accommodations) concern—and it has been one of many instructors with whom I've spoken over the years. Of course, I share this concern. However, a savvy instructor can work with these kinds of concerns—there are software programs available that allow a teacher to glance at the screens of the students from his/her own console screen and send messages of warning to stay on task. I have used one or two of these tools in the past, including the DyKnow classroom management software. This type of product can also be used to some positive effect to prevent cheating on in-class tests, which could provide a way for teachers in larger

classes to implement across-the-board laptop access. In fact, in any setting, access to the internet can be disabled for a certain period of time or
the whole class, if requested. This is similar to what some schools provide
for students with DSS accommodations when they're taking in-class tests:
an internet-disabled laptop. Steve (a student who does receive accommodations) mentioned that, at his current institution, he is often given such a
tool to take tests, since he is granted the opportunity to type his responses
on assessments.

Steve's experience and opinion lead to a concern that he has, which is
that perhaps not all students should be offered accommodations. He questions whether the level playing field that accommodations are designed to
provide would, indeed, still be level if everyone got the accommodations.
He does not believe that accommodations should be offered to all students,
because "the accommodation is intended to level the playing field and provide students with learning and/or physical disabilities the opportunity to
produce their best work, which truly would not be possible for them to
do otherwise." Even with Steve's physical disability, he types slowly—it's
a symptom of his fine-motor-skills problem. If others without that disability are also allowed to use the computer, Steve points out, they would
potentially type faster than others and thus could write more in the same
amount of time. If essay length were valued by teachers or scorers, that
would then give the non-disabled student a further advantage. Of course,
this is the case anyway—some students think and write (and type) faster
than others. One would assume that the typing would benefit everyone, but
not necessarily. But then perhaps the students could get extended time on
such assessments, which is another reasonable accommodation that is commonly afforded to students in certain situations. Georgie also pointed out
that there is a sense that giving accommodations to everyone might not be
fair for people who truly need them, that it would be as if they were taking
advantage of the teacher.

Interestingly, however, Donna, who also has the accommodation to
use a computer to take notes and tests, doesn't take advantage of that one,
because, she says, "I hate computers and I write faster then [sic] I type. It
would help with spelling but I hate computers!! I am getting better though
so I decided to keep that on the list, maybe one day I will use it." In fact,
Donna chose to hand-write her survey answers rather than type them out.
For her part, Donna does not have an issue with all students being offered
accommodations, because, she says, it could help them get a better grade.

> I think everyone has a LD even a little bit. Mine is just more noticable[sic]. . . . I think all the accommdations [sic] should be offered to all students – not just certain ones, with permission [sic] of the instructor of course.

Donna's point brings to mind one of my own students. I didn't interview this student (or any of my own students), but in office hours recently, he commented about using computers in the classroom—he's a slow typist and worries about getting everything done in class. (If it's not obvious already, I allow all my students to use their university-issued laptops in class for in-class writing exercises.) He says he does not have a diagnosed disability and thus is not working with the DSS office, so I told him to simply let me know if he needed any more time to complete an in-class writing assignment and I would give him extra time (beyond class time) to submit. I don't know if he would have even brought this up if we were not chatting one-on-one outside of the classroom. This brings up the very important issue of students who are not diagnosed or who have not self-disclosed and who might benefit from this kind of accommodation. Much has been written about disclosure of hidden disabilities; suffice it to say that, as Alexandrin et al have pointed out,

> though they will acknowledge that there are advantages to people being unaware of their disability, like not having low expectations inflicted upon them [see Nick, below] or not being stared at, the risk and fear people with hidden disabilities face over needing to disclose often outweigh the comfort of their invisibility. (377–78)

Yet another student concern revealed by the surveys focused on the notion of extensions. One non-diagnosed student, Michaela, wondered whether blanket extensions are appropriate or helpful. To explain, she pointed out that extensions that are given a day or two before an essay is due because several people asked the professor for an extension can be considered unfair and even off-putting. In her case, she gauges her other work according to assignment due dates. If she has worked on that paper because it's due Friday and then finds out Thursday she has more time on it, that can be upsetting if, for example, she had given less attention to another class or another assignment because she had the Friday due date on the essay in question. If she had known earlier that she would have had more time, then she might have been able to give better time to other projects or assignments or meetings or clubs or her other commitments. My best response to this concern is to explain, vis-à-vis due dates, that students can be given blanket notice that anyone who needs an extension is welcome to ask for one, with sufficient time before the due date—at least 24 hours is my normal practice.

This way no individual or group is unfairly advantaged or disadvantaged, and it allows the individual student's academic situation to remain a private matter between the student and the professor.

On the other hand, the students who had been diagnosed with one or more learning or other disabilities said they liked the idea that, if everyone were given accommodations, it might be less obvious that they were the few in the class with the so-called learning disabilities. Some students described feeling embarrassed, at first, by being highlighted (either intentionally or unintentionally) by a teacher endeavoring to make their accommodations available to them. Both Georgie and Donna mention the stigma factor (Georgie's term) associated with being a student with official accommodations. Donna points out that she wishes more professors had training in how to deal with accommodations—she says that she's had professors who didn't know what accommodations were, and, on the other hand, she has had a

> few instructors say in front of the class, I think without thinking, not wanting to cause a problem, '[Donna] don't forget the test in the LD office.' That's embrassing [sic]—now the entire class knows. I think if all students were allowed accommdations [sic] I wouldn't have to worry about all the list [of accommodations] above. We would fit more in[sic].

In that vein, Saima described situations where students with learning disabilities actually helped the whole class, such as when an assignment wasn't clear. In that event, if the LD students asked for more clarity, they and everyone else got the improved information or response from the professor or teaching assistant. This observation points to the idea that UDL-based assignments are good for all students, not just students with so-called learning disabilities.

The literature reflecting the student perspective on this particular issue—accommodations for all students in the writing classroom—appears rather thin. Most of it focuses on learning disabled students who were commenting on their experiences in the general college classroom, not necessarily a writing classroom. However, in "Learning Differences: The Perspective of LD Students" by Patricia Dunn, I was particularly struck by Nick, an LD student who, when asked about dos and don'ts for teachers, pointed out the following:

> I guess there's numerous dos and don'ts, but probably the number one don't would be to look at [students with learning disabilities] differently—because a student usually is uncomfortable with their disability anyway, and any time a teacher almost looks down upon them

and says, 'You don't have to do this quality of work because you have a disability,' that, in my mind, says that they don't think that we can do the work, so therefore they're not making us do the work. Therefore, they set a lower standard, and that perpetuates a continuously low quality of work. I see that happen continuously in high school as well as college. (149)

This is a very important perspective, and one that should make all teachers—and writing teachers in particular—pause and think about how we deal with our expectations of all of our students, whether learning disabled or not.

As Godden and Womack point out in "Combatting Inaccessible Spaces and Logics,"

this debate is about more than the best way to take notes. It is about the assumptions instructors make about students. It's about the narratives educators construct about learning. All too often, underlying discussions of appropriate student behavior and traditional best practices are narrow visions of students' abilities and classroom praxis. Seeing a study [sic] body as an undifferentiated group leads to strict rules and single solutions. (n.pag.)

Is it an overstatement to claim that this discussion is an issue of human decency and ethical treatment of students? Of what benefit is it to be hesitant about offering accommodations to everyone or discouraging students from asking for favors or breaks? What is the harm of setting up situations in which students can actually learn to write better? There must be ways of making accommodations available to all students that are still deferential to the ways we make specialized accommodations available for differently abled students. And, has been mentioned, the generally-offered accommodations might even help non-diagnosed LD students or students who have hidden their disabilities, which could be an excellent unintended outcome. According to the National Council on Disability, about eleven percent of undergraduates have a disability —however, how many of us can say with confidence that we have even ten percent of self-disclosing diagnosed students in our classrooms? There must be many students who are going unnoticed and are thus potentially unserved.

There are reasonable concerns that could be and have been expressed regarding these ideas; some of them are based on academic freedom, some are based on access, and some are based on comfort level, among other issues. Certainly many faculty lack a comfort level with introducing these ideas into their classrooms. As Donna said above, teachers need to be trained. Of course there is the issue of academic freedom—faculty should be allowed to teach in the ways that work for them. Generally speaking, no one would decry a faculty member's reliance on print media or hand-written notes—it is the stuff of traditional education. But I would submit that writing faculty need to consider rethinking their reliance on what John Jones, in his article, "The Situational Approach to Learning with New Media," calls "the nostalgia approach" to teaching with (or without) media (Jones), and I would extend his ideas to teaching with accommodations. He says that "to the extent that electronic devices do not fit in *that* cultural context . . . they are considered bad (for society/kids)." And surely, not all students—or faculty—have access to the electronic devices (the technology) that open opportunities for writing. But this is changing. Many students with and without so-called disabilities have access to, for example, laptop computers and smartphones.

Jones would add that some faculty, as they relate to technology use (or avoidance), are focused on the "work habits approach," which implies that people do their best work by following certain habits—but he contends that it is "important to not let habits close us off to new opportunities for learning" (n. pag.). He ultimately suggests a "situational approach," which "is respectful of the other two approaches, while simultaneously clear-eyed about the potential benefits (and drawbacks) of new technologies" and new ways of teaching. He points out that "when it comes to learning, we should be always open to questioning our own processes and assumptions, particularly as the material and social conditions of our learning change." (Jones). This should extend to teaching. It would be my recommendation that writing faculty should constantly consider, situationally, what types of accommodations can work in their classrooms. Academic freedom means nothing if it, in effect, imprisons students in the professor's ideal world.

Indeed, what about the students? Who speaks for the students? I believe that students want to write better and teachers want to teach writing better. Perhaps some of the ideas expressed herein could be a start. From the perspective of access to technology, these ideas are admittedly based on a few important premises, and not all WPAs, writing teachers, and even students are at a place (literally and figuratively) in their teaching/learning careers, in their programs, and/or in their institutions to fully embrace these tenets. Indeed, these philosophies of teaching/learning probably require writing faculty to consider whether the following principles are realistic in their settings:

1. Writing classes are small (no more than 20 people).

2. Students have laptops or other mobile devices—or access to them.

3. Students and teachers are comfortable with technology.

4. Teachers are aware of their own disabilities, biases, pet peeves, hang-ups, and are willing to work with them—or let them go, if necessary.

5. Teachers value kindness and are willing to help students learn and succeed rather than expecting them to do it alone. (It's important, as some teachers instead value toughness—and for good reasons.)

6. Teachers want to reflect and improve.

7. Teachers want to reach more students.

Certainly as WPAs and writing teachers we should regularly reflect on our practice. As noted by Juli Kramer in her article, "A Deweyan Reflection," we need to see problems from a different perspective. She contends that, by

> engaging in a methodical process [of reflection], teachers can examine and think about choices, methods, experiences, and other aspects of classroom life in order to uncover and understand what works, what does not, and perhaps identify paradigms that put up barriers to more effective learning (76).

In fact, I have come to realize that some of my so-called accommodations, which I thought were so helpful, might not be. The practice of allowing all students laptop access is a critical one at my university, as all undergraduate students are issued laptops as part of their academic programs. Many faculty do not allow laptops in the classrooms. I do—and require their use. However, I can think of situations (as have been described herein) in almost all of my classes where, even though everyone is typing, one or two students still took a while to type out their responses to, say, an in-class writing prompt. In this case, I can see where allowing everyone to have a laptop in the classroom may not be helpful. Maybe those students type slowly, maybe they take a while to compose their thoughts, maybe they struggle to do on-call writing/typing. Certainly if they asked me for more time or to post their response later, I would allow it, but it's interesting, nonetheless, to realize that the laptop may not actually help everyone. And yet for some people it's critical.

I also find myself thinking about whether I give too many accommodations—in other words, if a student has only certain accommodations on his/her list, do I give the student the benefit of the doubt in other areas just because I have a DSS letter? Do I expect less of her/him? Or does that just feed into my theory of giving everyone everything I can give, assuming it will help a lot of people and hoping it won't hurt anyone?

Ultimately, this pedagogical work rests on the idea of giving. When we teach, we are giving students us, and they are giving us them. In talking about the classroom as a home, where the teacher is hospitable to her/his students, Kramer gives life to students/guests:

> They are people with their own worth, experiences, and feelings. Teachers will always have the responsibility to control and shape student behavior and their classroom experience, but by putting on the lens of hospitality and kindness, they reframe how they work within and use their authority. (83)

It seems that, in our own ways, if we can be kind, inclusive, and understanding—while still challenging our students in the process—we can help our students learn through and about writing. They might become better writers—and we might become better teachers.

NOTES

1. All names are pseudonyms. This research was determined to be exempt from IRB-required approval.

APPENDIX A: QUESTIONNAIRE: ACCOMMODATIONS IN THE WRITING CLASSROOM

1) How many years of college have you completed? If you've graduated, when did you graduate and with what degree?

2) As a high school or college student, were you diagnosed with one or more learning, emotional, or physical disabilities?

3) If so, and if you feel comfortable sharing, which one(s)?

4) If you were not so diagnosed (or even if you were), did you know anyone in high school or college who was diagnosed with such disabilities? Do you know which ones?

5) If you did have such a diagnosis or if you did know people with such diagnoses, what accommodations did you receive (or are you aware others received) in classes that featured a significant amount of writing (two or more essays or papers)? These accommodations might have been untimed essay tests, extended time on papers, use of a computer in the classroom, and so on. Please list and any all accommodations that you either received and/or that you're aware that others received.

6) If you did receive such accommodations or knew people who did, how helpful (as far as you know) were these accommodations to the

students' academic achievement? Please describe how helpful they were as best you can.

7) As far as you know, were these accommodations not helpful? Please describe, as best you can, how they were not helpful.

8) Have you ever received such accommodations in a writing class without being asked if you needed and/or wanted them? If so, which accommodations and what is your opinion about that experience?

9) Do you think that accommodations for differently abled students should be offered to all students – at least those that involve writing? Why or why not?

10) If you think accommodations should be universally offered, do you think all accommodations should be offered or just certain ones? If just certain ones, which ones would be appropriate for all students?

11) Is there anything else about your (or others') experiences with accommodations in the writing classroom that you would like to share or add to what you've said above?

Works Cited

Alexandrin, Julie R., Ilana Lyn Schreiber, and Elizabeth Henry. "Why Not Disclose?" *Pedagogy and Student Services for Institutional Transformation: Implementing Universal Design in Higher Education*. Edited by Jeanne L. Higbee and Emily Goff, University of Minnesota, 2008, pp. 377–90.

Bowe, Frank G. "Introduction and Executive Summary." *Universal Design in Education: Teaching Nontraditional Students*. Bergin & Garvey, 2000, pp. 1–6.

Conference on College Composition and Communication. "Principles for the Postsecondary Teaching of Writing." CCCC Position Statement, National Council of Teachers of English, March 2015.

Dolmage, Jay. "Mapping Composition: Inviting Disability in the Front Door." *Disability and the Teaching of Writing: A Critical Sourcebook*, edited by Cynthia Lewiecki-Wilson, Brenda Jo Brueggemann, Jay Dolmage, Bedford/St. Martin's, 2008, pp. 14–27.

Donna. Interview. 12 October 2016.

Dunn, Patricia A. "Learning Differences: The Perspective of LD College Students." *Disability and the Teaching of Writing: A Critical Sourcebook*, edited by Cynthia Lewiecki-Wilson, Brenda Jo Brueggemann, Jay Dolmage, Bedford/St. Martin's, 2008, pp. 147–52.

Georgie. Interview. 18 June 2016.

Godden, Rick, and Anne-Marie Womack. "Making Disability Part of the Conversation: Combatting Inaccessible Space and Logics." *Hybrid Pedagogy: A Digital*

Journal of Learning, Teaching, and Scholarship. Digital Pedagogy Lab, 12 May 2016.

Jones, John. "The Situational Approach to Learning with New Media." *Digital Media +Learning: The Power of Participation*. DML Central. August 18, 2016.

Kevin. Interview. 10 October 2016.

Kramer, Julie. "A DEWEYAN REFLECTION: The Potential of Hospitality and Movement in the Classroom," *Curriculum and Teaching Dialogue*. Information Age Publishing, 2016, pp. 75–87.

Michaela. Interview. 18 June 2016.

National Council on Disability (NCD). "Briefing Paper: Reauthorization of the Higher Education Act (HEA): The Implications for Increasing the Employment of People with Disabilities." NCD. 15 May 2015.

Nielsen, Danielle. "Universal Design in First-Year Composition—Why Do We Need It? Can We Do It?" *CEA Forum*, vol. 42, no. 2, 2013, pp. 3–29.

Paul, Annie Murphy. "Are College Lectures Unfair?" *Sunday Review. New York Times,* 12 Sept. 2015.

Roberts, Kelly D., Hye Jin Park, Steven Brown, and Bryan Cook. "Universal Design for Instruction in Postsecondary Education: A Systematic Review of Empirically Based Articles." *Journal of Postsecondary Education and Disability*, vol. 24, no. 1, 2011, pp. 5–15.

Saima. Interview. 18 June 2016.

Stes, Ana, and Peter Van Petegem. "Profiling Approaches to Teaching in Higher Education: A Cluster-Analytic study." *Studies in Higher Education*, vol. 39, no. 4, 2014, pp. 644–58.

Steve. Interview. 21 October 2016.

Kelly A. Shea is an associate professor of English and director of the First-Year Writing Program at Seton Hall University, a four-year private Roman Catholic university. She is a co-leader of the university's Core Curriculum Reading- and Writing- Intensive Proficiency initiative and works closely with faculty throughout her department and the university on the effective use of course management systems, on improving faculty development, on creative assessment, and on other pedagogy-improvement initiatives. She teaches undergraduate and graduate composition and literature courses and studies writing, teaching, and technology, and their intersections.

Review

Developing Inclusive and Accessible Online Writing Instruction: Supporting OWI Principle 1

Brenta Blevins

Coombs, Norman. *Making Online Teaching Accessible: Inclusive Course Design for Students with Disabilities*. Jossey-Bass, 2010. 192 pages.

This text is also available in a Large Print edition from ReadHowYouWant, 2012. 264 pages.

In response to the rise in online writing instruction, the CCCC OWI Committee released in 2013 *A Position Statement of Principles and Example Effective Practices for Online Writing Instruction (OWI)*. The statement's first principle is: "Online writing instruction should be universally inclusive and accessible." With growing numbers of students taking online instruction—more than one in four students enrolled in an online course in 2014 (Allen and Seaman 12)—and given that eleven percent of college students reported having disabilities in 2012 (US Department of Education), the need exists for making online writing instruction accessible and inclusive. Preceding the development of the CCCC OWI Committee's 2013 position statement, Norman Coombs' *Making Online Teaching Accessible: Inclusive Course Design for Students with Disabilities* provides helpful guidance to instructors, instructional designers, information technology staff, student disability services staff, and administrators for supporting accessible OWI. A blind, Black scholar, Coombs draws from his own experiences and expertise as student, instructor, and learning technologist to reconceptualize difference and advocate accessibility as an advantage to all. Although published seven years ago, this book is an enduring volume that focuses on concepts important for supporting the CCCC OWI Principle 1. Coombs' book presents a reassuring approach by having faculty use the "everyday content-authoring applications that faculty are already familiar with—such as Microsoft Word," resulting in implementing accessible content more easily, and less expensively, than feared (x).

Coombs helpfully identifies early what accessibility is and why it matters. In the preface, he defines accessibility as providing online course content that "can be effectively used by people who fall into the following disability groups" and lists students who are blind, have severe visual impairments but are not legally blind; students who have upper body motor impairments; students with either visual or cognitive processing difficulties; and students with hearing impairments (x). Coombs provides administrators and instructors arguments for why accessibility matters, pointing out that in US society, "we have decided that providing access to public buildings and transportation for people who are unable to walk is the right thing to do," and have created building codes and laws to support that decision (xii). Such decisions have extended to the educational realm (10–15), although Coombs notes that educational equal access has lagged (xii). As Webster Newbold points out in *Foundational Practices of Online Writing Instruction*, however, "it is our institutions' legal responsibility and ours as employees to make appropriate accommodations under the Americans with Disabilities Act (ADA) of 1990 (see also Section 504 of the Rehabilitation Act of 1973)" (xiii). Coombs' book helps instructors and administrators meet these responsibilities in online courses.

Making Online Teaching Accessible resides at the intersection of two writing instruction-focused conversations: OWI and disability. Online writing instruction has been addressed by Scott Warnock, Beth Hewett, and Hewett and Kevin Eric DePew, as well as others. Scholars, such as Sushil K. Oswal, Melanie Yergeau, Jay Dolmage, Stephanie L. Kerschbaum, and Margaret Price (works by Dolmage, Kerschbaum, and Price are also reviewed in this special issue), and resources, such as *Disability and the Teaching of Writing: A Critical Sourcebook*, have brought increasing attention to issues of disability in writing classes. These conversations have been addressed in combination in Oswal's "Physical and Learning Disabilities in OWI" while Hewett provides some discussion of accessibility in *The Online Writing Conference: A Guide for Teachers and Tutors*. Although not specifically a writing instruction-focused text, *Making Online Teaching Accessible* is an important addition. Coombs' combined attention to access and online instruction is detailed and approachable, even for individuals without extensive technical expertise.

The majority of *Making Online Teaching Accessible* focuses on faculty, primarily in helping instructors develop accessible online courses. Coombs begins with descriptions of students, describing how people with disabilities use computers through such tools as voice recognition technology, on-screen keyboards, screen magnification software, screen readers, and audio transcriptions and video captioning, which student disability services staff can help students use. Such perspective is helpful in understanding the students who may enroll in online courses.

The majority of the book's chapters focus broadly on developing accessible course content. Citing the American Foundation for the Blind (2008), Coombs offers that accessibility depends on "three 'legs' of the online learning tripod": accessibility of the learning management system (LMS), accessibility of the actual course content, and the skill of the student in using up-to-date assistive technology" (19). Instructors can support the second leg of accessible course content by incorporating such characteristics as consistent designs and accessible graphics (24). Coombs includes additional practical advice, such as modularizing and organizing course content into bite-size chunks, providing a text equivalent for every non-text element (for instance, when including images—which he advocates inclusion of for students who learn better with visuals—incorporating also a textual description for screen readers), including captions for multimedia presentations, applying color carefully, and using headers to make data tables accessible (24–28).

A design focus facilitates implementation of accessible content. Universal design enables "products and environments to be usable by all people, to the greatest extent possible, without the need for adaptation or specialized design" (Connell et al). Coombs provides an overview of universal design, the goal of which

> when applied to education is to make learning inclusive for all students, not just those with disabilities. It is an approach to designing all products and services to be usable by students with the widest possible range of both functional (physical) capabilities and different learning styles. (7)

For example, in providing instructions on how instructors can create narrated slide shows, which simulate an instructor delivering traditional classroom talks, Coombs states that although narrated presentations will cause few problems for most individuals with disabilities, people with hearing impairments will have trouble; including a transcript accompanying the video provides a means for individuals to access that content. Applying these universal design principles using familiar authoring tools "is not a burden" in creating accessible content (Coombs 124). The universal design approach supports Coombs' contention that the "first step in advancing online content accessibility is improving your quality of teaching and the clarity of your communication for everyone, including students with disabilities" (124).

In articulating how instructors can develop accessible course content, Coombs demonstrates that instructors can utilize their familiarity with such tools as Microsoft Office in chapters Three and Four. Here, Coombs identifies features to avoid because of their incompatibility with assistive technology—although he notes that assistive technologies may support them in the future. Coombs carefully walks readers through concepts like making content accessible using such software as Microsoft Office and Camtasia's video maker, addressing specifically such tasks as creating narration in PowerPoint and publishing formatted files through Word. One inevitable outcome from this specific description is that software changes rapidly, and thus some step-by-step instructions and images do not precisely match those in more recent software versions. However, despite such minor discrepancies, the book's conceptual presentation remains highly relevant, and readers can accomplish the described software activities through minor adaptation. Coombs additionally provides information on a number of resources throughout the text, pointing readers to such tools as the WAVE Web accessibility evaluation tool, available online and through browser extensions, and also includes an extensive Resources list after the Appendices. Throughout, Coombs' software discussion demonstrates accessible content can be made through the software tools with which instructors are already familiar.

The last chapter addresses the need for institution-wide support of online instruction accessibility and inclusion. Such support should be provided for students with disabilities taking online courses; faculty and instructional design staff developing online course content; and IT staff responsible for the LMS and supporting faculty learning and using it (Coombs 118). Coombs argues for an integrated, campus-wide support team. Accessible online learning requires more than just committed instructors and administrators; it also requires institutional support and input across the campus, particularly as some concerns cannot be addressed by instructors alone. For example, accessible courses require not only having an LMS that is itself accessible, but also that any pages required for the student to navigate to the LMS and any pages housing content must also be accessible. An institutional structure enables faculty and staff to support each other in supporting students. With their discussions of legal responsibilities and a proposed campus structure, the first and last chapters best support administrative considerations for supporting online course accessibility.

Covering the range of LMS software, course content development, legislation, and student populations, *Making Online Teaching Accessible* makes clear that having accessible, inclusive courses means having multiple individuals working together toward this shared goal. Building upon the familiar—that is, instructors' familiarity with using tools in Microsoft Office—makes accessibility easier, and less expensive, than many might fear. With its clear, concise text, consistent headings, legible typeface, and bite-sized chunks and summaries, the book itself demonstrates the kind of design principles that Coombs recommends for accessible online courses. Administrators at both programmatic and institutional levels, online course instructors, IT, and student disability support staff can look to Norman Coombs's *Making Online Teaching Accessible: Inclusive* for guidance on developing and supporting online writing courses that provide the accessibility that US law and the OWI Principle 1 require.

Works Cited

American Foundation for the Blind. "Distance Learning: How Accessible are Online Educational Tools," American Foundation for the Blind, 2008, www.afb.org/info/programs-and-services/public-policy-center/technology-and-information-accessibility/distance-learning-how-accessible-are-online-educational-tools-4492/1235.

Allen, I. Elaine, and Jeff Seaman with Russell Poulin and Terri Taylor Straut. "2015 Online Report Card - Tracking Online Education in the United States," Online Learning Consortium, 2015, onlinelearningconsortium.org/read/online-report-card-tracking-online-education-united-states-2015.

Brueggeman, Brenda, and Cindy Lewiecki-Wilson, editors. *Disability and the Teaching of Writing: A Critical Sourcebook.* Bedford St. Martin's, 2006.

CCCC OWI Committee for Effective Practices in Online Writing Instruction. "A Position Statement of Principles and Effective Practices for Online Writing Instruction (OWI)," 2013, www.ncte.org/cccc/resources/ positions/owiprinciples.

Center for Universal Design. Center for Universal Design, 2008, www.ncsu.edu/ncsu/design/cud/.

Connell, Bettye Rose, Mike Jones, Ron Mace, Jim Mueller, Abir Mullick, Elaine Ostroff, Jon Sanford, Ed Steinfeld, Molly Story, and Gregg Vanderheiden. "The Principles of Universal Design." *Center for Universal Design*, NC State University, 1997.

Dolmage, Jay. "Disability Studies Pedagogy, Usability and Universal Design." *Disability Studies Quarterly*, vol. 25, no. 4, 2005.

—. "Universal Design: Places to Start." *Disability Studies Quarterly*, vol. 35, no. 2, 2015.

Hewett, Beth L. *Reading to Learn and Writing to Teach: Literacy Strategies for Online Writing Instruction.* Bedford/St. Martin's, 2015.

—. *The Online Writing Conference: A Guide for Teachers and Tutors.* Bedford/St Martin's, 2015.

Hewett, Beth L, and Kevin E. DePew, editors. *Foundational Practices of Online Writing Instruction*. With Elif Guler and Robbin Zeff Warner, The WAC Clearinghouse; Parlor Press, 2015.

Newbold, Webster. "Preface." Hewett and DePew, pp. xi–xv.

Oswal, Sushil. "Physical and Learning Disabilities in OWI." Hewett and DePew, pp. 253–89.

US Department of Education, National Center for Education Statistics. "Students with Disabilities." Institute of Education Sciences, nces.ed.gov/fastfacts/display.asp?id=60.

Warnock, Scott. *Teaching Writing Online: How and Why*. NCTE, 2009.

WAVE Web Accessibility Evaluation Tool. WebAIM, wave.webaim.org/.

Wood, Tara, Jay Dolmage, Margaret Price, and Cynthia Lewiecki-Wilson. "Where We Are: Disability and Accessibility: Moving Beyond Disability 2.0 in Composition Studies." *Composition Studies* vol. 42, no. 2, 2014, pp. 147–50.

Yergeau, Melanie, Elizabeth Brewer, Stephanie Kerschbaum, Sushil K. Oswal, Margaret Price, Cynthia L. Selfe, Michael J. Salvo, and Franny Howes. "Multimodality in Motion: Disability and *Kairotic* Spaces," *Kairos: A Journal of Rhetoric, Technology, and Pedagogy* vol. 18, no. 1, 2013, kairos.technorhetoric.net/18.1/coverweb/yergeau-et-al/index.html.

Brenta Blevins completed her PhD in English/Rhetoric and Composition at the University of North Carolina at Greensboro. Her research focuses on writing for emerging media, multimodality, and digital literacy.

Review

Rereading and Retelling Rhetoric's Embodied Stories

Ella R. Browning

Dolmage, Jay Timothy. *Disability Rhetoric*. Syracuse University Press, 2014. 349 pages.

A powerful and exciting project for those readers in rhetoric and writing studies who are familiar with disability studies, Jay Dolmage's *Disability Rhetoric* offers an accessible entry into this important conversation for readers from a range of backgrounds with either disability studies or rhetoric and writing studies, from undergraduates to senior scholars. *Disability Rhetoric* asks us consider what kinds of disability futures might be possible if we reconsider our understandings of rhetoric, disability, and, at their intersections, disability rhetoric, all through disability historiography and disability futures. Put another way, in *Disability Rhetoric* Dolmage asks critical questions of the stories we have told about certain bodies, the stories we have ignored, and the stories that need to be retold. Importantly, he gives readers the tools to continue asking these kinds of critical questions and to teach our students to do so as well.

Part historical, part theoretical, and part applied rhetorical analysis, *Disability Rhetoric* argues that we can and should reread bodied rhetorical history and embodied rhetoric as powered by an ongoing and longstanding tension around notions of normativity. Through such a disability historiography, we might re/shape potential disability futures. The introduction, "Prothesis," provides readers with an overview of the book, its structure, and a preview of some of Dolmage's central arguments. In chapter 1, on "Disability Studies of Rhetoric," Dolmage explores the rhetorical history of the disability studies concept of normativity, drawing on the work of disability studies scholars such as Martha Rose and Lennard Davis and scholars of rhetoric such as Andrea Lunsford and Susan Jarratt, among others. In chapter 2, "Rhetorical Histories of Disability," Dolmage turns his attention to the classical roots of the field of rhetoric and asks that we "expand our ideas about who our rhetorical teachers might be, and what types of intelligence they might valorize, as well as what forms this intelligence might take in body and mind (always together) in action" (67). Chapter 3, "Imperfect Meaning," examines the ways that disability has been constructed and defined as deficit, as well as proposed models and theories of disability as unique, imperfect, powerful, and meaning-making.

Chapter 4, "*Métis,*" is one of the book's most important chapters, focusing on the mythical stories of the disabled Greek god Hephaestus, "his craft, his cunning, his ability" (193) and challenging commonly held perceptions about this figure. Chapter 5, "Eating Rhetorical Bodies," continues the work of chapter 4 and looks at the figure of Metis, the Greek goddess named after *métis*, the form of intelligence, alongside mythical and rhetorical retellings of *métis* myths, notably Helene Cixous' use of the Medusa myths and Gloria Anzaldua's *mestizaje*, among others. In Chapter 6, "I Did It on Purpose," Dolmage focuses on the Oscar-winning film, *The King's Speech* because it is both a movie about rhetoric and a movie about disability, as a space in which to apply the questions and ideas of the book in order to argue that such questions and ideas "have real, contemporary significance" (225). Finally, in the book's conclusion, or "Prosthesis," Dolmage considers the stories the book has told and the future stories that the book might help readers tell about disability rhetoric. Among the progression of these chapters Dolmage has also included two interchapters, an innovative new genre that provides useful and quite powerful takeaways for readers to apply to their own classrooms, writing programs, and scholarship.

The two interchapters Dolmage includes in *Disability Rhetoric* are worth discussing here in depth because of the important accessibility they provide for readers new to the field of disability studies. The first, located after chapter 1 and titled "Archive and Anatomy of Disability Myths," charts persistent disability myths in order to demonstrate the ways that disability is rhetorically shaped. Dolmage provides a chart constructed of three columns—Myth, Description, and Example—and traces a range of disability myths, such as Physical Deformity as Sign of Internal Flaw, Disability as Isolating and Individuated, and Disability as a Sign of Social Issue through a variety of contemporary and historical rhetorical artifacts, including novels, speeches, films, and the Bible. Of particular use in this section is what Dolmage describes as the "Disability Myth 'Test'." Similar to the Bechdel Test, developed by Alison Bechdel as a way to interrogate how female characters are positioned in a movie, Dolmage proposes versions of a Disability Myth Test to interrogate how disability is positioned in a movie and asks that readers continue to problematize and theorize such a test and the texts to which we could apply it. This test, along with Dolmage's broader list of disability myths, would be a useful way of introducing undergraduate students to a disability studies perspective they might turn on the cultural texts they consume in their everyday lives.

The second interchapter, located after chapter 4 and titled "Repertoire and Choreography of Disability Rhetorics," proposes a range of disability rhetorics: "means of conceptualizing not just how meaning is attached to disability, but to view the knowledge and meaning that disability *generates*" (125). Contrasting his inventory against that of the *Diagnostic and Statistical Manual of Mental Disorders* (DSM), Dolmage describes this work as labeling a range of conditions–in this case, rhetorical conditions–but in a way that frames them as potential rather than deficit (126). Recalling Jeanne Fahnestock's definition of rhetorical figures as departures from the expected order of words, Dolmage extends this definition further and argues that "in this way, all rhetorical figures are nonnormative or 'disabled': they are the abnormality that fires newness and invites novel and multiple interpretations" (126). The rhetorical figures Dolmage includes in this interchapter, then, have the potential to generate nonnormative meanings, and Dolmage provides examples of how to do this kind of reinterpretive work so that readers might adapt, activate, and make their own meanings. Much like the chart Dolmage includes in his first interchapter, this inventory of disability rhetorics is also in the form of a chart with three columns: Rhetoric, Description, and Example. Dolmage's full list is too comprehensive to include here, but one example can demonstrate the usefulness and importance of this addition to the book.

Describing Situated Knowledges as "an elaboration of the concept of standpoint epistemology," and recalling Donna Haraway's explanation that "subjugated standpoints are preferred because they seem to promise more adequate, sustained, objective, transforming accounts of the world" (191), Dolmage provides the following explanation of how we might consider disability as situated knowledge framed with an emphasis on potential rather than deficit: "One example of disability as 'situated knowledge' offering a 'transformative account' of the world is that many of the technologies developed first for people with disabilities (such as optional character recognition texting, or email) have reshaped communication for all" (130). This simple shift in perspective is a powerful one, and one that could be particularly useful when deployed in the classroom. How else might we take rhetorical figures and re/figure them taking into account the potential of disability for generative meaning-making? How else might we reread embodied rhetorical strategies as disability rhetoric?

One of Dolmage's central arguments is that the body has never been fully or fairly understood for its role in shaping and multiplying our understanding of rhetoric as deploying every available means of persuasion. Some bodies were neglected from the story of rhetoric's beginnings while others (or, "Others"), like those with disabilities, were positioned as arhetorical through which discourses on rhetoric were shaped. Exceptions to this arhetoricity were figures Dolmage identifies as super crip, a disability myth Dolmage expands on in interchapter 1 and traces from Greek mythology through contemporary texts. He expands on his goals by explaining:

> An emphasis on rhetorical embodiment, when coupled with this disability studies perspective, offers ways to interrogate how our ideas about bodily norms have conditioned our experience of rhetoric and offers ways to analyze how and why, and to what effect, we have projected our visions, feelings, and experiences of rhetoric into this narrow, nearly fictional world, invested in a particular kind of body, imprisoned in the geometry of the norm. We may never fully escape this normative conditioning, but we can engage with the ongoing work of critical realignment. The first step is to recognize the *canon* of bodily denigration and then to begin shaking it, both from within the specific rhetorical histories we have chosen and from without. (71; emphasis original)

Throughout *Disability Rhetoric*, Dolmage returns to the stories that make up rhetoric's canon and shakes them out. In so doing, he also asks us to shift the ways that we consider the rhetorical implications of contemporary texts, and offers readers critical tools through which to do so.

While not every first year writing seminar or writing program includes attention to disability rhetoric, perhaps it should. In fact, perhaps all postsecondary writing and rhetoric instruction should attend to disability rhetoric in some way, from content-focused discussions to critical approaches to assignment design (see also the review in this volume by Annika Konrad for examples of how a politics of wonder uncovers unexamined assumptions about disability in classrooms and writing programs). As I have written about here already, one of the most engaging and compelling aspects of *Disability Rhetoric* is that it is filled with stories: stories of Greek gods and goddesses, stories of classical philosophers and mythical figures, stories on the screen, stories on the page, stories we tell ourselves, stories we have forgotten, and stories we have ignored. Most importantly, in asking us to re/consider the stories of where rhetoric and disability, and the intersections of the two, have come from, Dolmage also asks us to re/consider the future of stories of disability rhetoric. In his "Prosthesis" to *Disability Rhet-*

oric, Dolmage writes, *"Métis* is a model for adaptation, change, critique, uniqueness, prosthesis, recursivity, invention, intercorporeality, ambiguity, and abstraction. What if these were our central educational values (instead of accumulation, retention, comprehension, compliance, reproduction)?" (289). We might extend this question one step further and ask, "What if these were our central cultural values?" *Disability Rhetoric* was published in 2014 but now, more than ever, these questions must be asked, especially as we work to shape the stories of our futures. Dolmage's concluding lines to *Disability Rhetoric* are powerful ones, and it seems fitting to use them here: "This book, like the 'even flame' of Hephaestus' metallurgy, might offer some illumination and heat. But it is up to you to forge and to adapt your own tools" (291). Luckily for the wide range of readers this book has likely already attracted, Dolmage has provided us with the means to do so.

Works Cited

Bechdel, Alison. *The Essential Dykes to Watch Out For.* New York: Houghton Mifflin Harcourt, 2008.

Davis, Lennard J. *Enforcing Normalcy: Disability, Deafness, and the Body.* New York: Verso, 1995.

Fahnestock, Jeanne. *Rhetorical Figures in Science.* Oxford University Press, 1999.

Haraway, Donna. "Situated Knowledges." In *Simians, Cyborgs, and Women: The Reinvention of Nature.* New York: Routledge, 1991.

Jarratt, Susan C. *Rereading the Sophists: Classical Rhetoric Refigured.* Carbondale: SIUP, 1991.

Lunsford, Andrea A., ed. *Reclaiming Rhetorica: Women in the Rhetorical Tradition.* Pittsburgh, U of Pittsburgh P, 1995.

Rose, Martha L. *The Staff of Oedipus: Transforming Disability in Ancient Greece.* Ann Arbor: U of Michigan P, 2003.

Ella R. Browning, PhD, is the Associate Director of Writing in the Disciplines in the Critical Writing Program at the University of Pennsylvania. She teaches and researches at the intersections of disability studies, professional and technical writing, feminist and queer theories, and health and medical rhetorics.

Review

Toward an Interpretive Framework for Access in Writing Programs

Annika Konrad

Titchkosky, Tanya. *The Question of Access: Disability, Space, Meaning.* University of Toronto Press, 2011. 192 pages.

> *"I've never had to deal with accessibility because I've never had a student with a disability in my class."*

> *"But I wasn't trained to deal with students with disabilities."*

> *"If a student's accommodations document asks for extended time on tests, but we're only writing papers, then I don't change anything."*

These are some of the claims I have heard instructors make about disability. In *The Question of Access: Disability, Space, Meaning*, Tanya Titchkosky argues that what is say-able about disability reflects our unexamined assumptions about what disability is and how access is created. The say-able things above, whether intentional or not, reflect disability as a visibly apparent problem found within an individual that needs to be treated using proper methods delivered by a bureaucratic entity. This is how universities often conceptualize disability, and it is through these means that students with disabilities receive accommodations. College instructors also depend on university services to address disability as an individual problem; for example, instructors are often required to include a statement in their syllabus that points students to disability resources, and they wait for students to present documentation that justifies individual accommodation. Titchkosky argues that relying solely on bureaucratic approaches to treat access on an individual basis makes disability an essentially excludable category of partial, maybe, contingent, not yet participants. Ultimately,

Titchkosky offers a conceptual framework that writing programs can use to move beyond bureaucratic approaches to access to practice interpretive approaches that involve constant, critical reflection upon relations between bodies and spaces.

Scholars in the field of Rhetoric and Composition/Writing Studies who research disability have also warned about the dangers of approaching disability as a bureaucratic matter. In "Where We Are: Disability and Accessibility," Tara Wood, Jay Dolmage, Margaret Price, and Cynthia Lewiecki-Wilson argue that checklists for accessibility reduce disability to an individualized problem that is "over there" (147). Instead, Wood et al advocate that disability should be perceived as an opportunity to experiment with our own practices like "adaptation, creativity, community, interdependency, technological ingenuity, and modal fluency" (148). Similarly, in "Suggested Practices for Syllabus Accessibility Statements," Shannon Madden and Tara Wood recommend that it is time to move beyond legal obligations for access. One way to do so is by recrafting our syllabus accessibility statements to reflect a more inclusive classroom space where access is co-constructed rather than only obtained through bureaucratic means. For similar arguments about other shortcomings of institutional conceptions of difference and the opportunities of relational, rhetorical approaches, see Kelly A. Whitney's review of Stephanie Kerschbaum's *Toward a New Rhetoric of Difference* and Elisabeth Miller's review of Margaret Price's *Mad at School: Rhetorics of Mental Disability and Academic Life*. What Titchkosky offers our field, however, is a rich, layered interpretive framework for critically interrogating our own assumptions about what disability is and where access lies. Titchkosky's framework moves access from the realm of bureaucracy to the realm of perception. By engaging Titchkosky's methodology of a politics of wonder, writing program leaders and instructors can critically examine their own perceptions of what disability is and where access lies. In doing so, we can use access as an interpretive lens for all that we do within writing programs.

A politics of wonder as Titchkosky defines it is a means of understanding access and disability as acts of perception or "a restless reflexive return to what has come before" (15). Engaging in a politics of wonder involves asking reflective questions about interpretive scenes of access. Titchkosky's book is comprised of interpretive scenes of access drawn from her experiences advocating for access in her role as a professor in the Department of Sociology and Equity Studies in Education at the University of Toronto. Repeatedly applying questions such as "Who needs access? What is disability? Where is disability? When is access?" to these interpretive scenes reveals countless assumptions about who belongs, when, where, and how in university life. Here I review a few examples of how a politics of wonder uncovers unexamined assumptions about disability, and I contextualize them within writing program administration.

Refiguring relations around access begins with the work of understanding what access is. The predominant understanding of access is that it is something that is granted or not, that either people have it or do not, and that it is something which can be arranged with appropriate policies, procedures, resources, tools, and documents. In other words, it is inherently tied to bureaucracy. While she recognizes that access does need to be legally protected and physically provided, Titchkosky argues that access also needs to be understood and questioned as interpretive relations between embodied experiences and the times, spaces, places, and social environments they inhabit. Access is an act of perception that orients our understandings of who does and does not belong in social space. People whose embodied experiences depart from what is naturally expected—such as people with disabilities—are perceived as less valued, less human, and in need of assistance and care. When we perceive disability as an individual problem, Titchkosky explains, we fail to notice the ways our perceptions naturalize only some bodies and some environments, making disabled people "justifiably excludable."

Interpretive scenes of access are often organized around cost and the quantification of bodies. Titchkosky recalls encountering these concerns in response to her efforts to use department grant money to build a flexible classroom space for up to forty students. She was met with a demand for information about who exactly will use this classroom because "you can't accommodate everybody." Examined through a politics of wonder, perceptions that insist upon "Who? Who will potentially be present? How many will actually need access?" reveal normative assumptions about "the ordinary shape of participation—the shape of the person and the shape of the space" (40). The danger of leaving assumptions about the relations between bodies and spaces unquestioned is that belonging is left to bureaucracy, and the effect is "actual bodies disappearing, becoming illusory background figures on the foreground of bureaucratic management" (39). While cost is likely also a concern for many writing programs, writing program leaders need to utilize their resources to maintain agency over "the shape of participation" (40). As scholars who have long been attuned to the socially situated nature of language and identity, we need to use our resources to avoid perpetuating the bureaucratic disappearance of people whose embodied experiences place them outside normative interpretive relations.

Questioning what we imagine disability to be is also imperative to engaging in a politics of wonder about access. One way to approach this is by examining the signs we use to signify access. Titchkosky takes the universal access sign (the white stick figure in a wheelchair on a blue background) as her case study. She tells a story about noticing signs of universal access in her workplace that mark doors that are too heavy, too narrow for wheelchairs to pass through, doors with automatic openers that lead to stairs, etc. When signs of access mark spaces that are not actually accessible, they construct disabled people as a "partially imagined may-be" (64). Like bureaucratic procedures that treat disability as a contingency, these misleading signs of access shape our collective imaginations of disabled people as partial participants. Writing program leaders and instructors need to engage in a politics of wonder about their own signs of access—e.g., syllabus accommodations statements, readings about disability, instructors' mentioning (or not) of disability resource centers, etc. As Madden and Wood ask, what message are we sending when we place information about disability resources at the bottom of our syllabi? What message are we sending when we speak only about disabled students in terms of accommodation? Or when we do nothing more than review accommodations guidelines with instructors in training? By asking ourselves these questions, we can begin to see how our own collective orientations toward disability "can also be made contingent – made into a maybe" (67).

In addition to critically examining what we imagine disability to be, we need to prevent the justification of the absence of access in our programs. Titchkosky demonstrates how disability appears "as a justified absence" in the ordinary exclusionary talk of her colleagues (70). Titchkosky lingers on one all-too-familiar say-able refrain relative to disability: "You know, I mean, things just weren't built with people with disabilities in mind" (73). Even if people disagree with these excuses for inaccessibility, "it remains an unexamined 'fact' of social life that it is reasonable to seek a reason for the lack of access" (77). The problem with giving reasons for inaccessibility is that it normalizes inaccessibility and conditions people to not even notice the absence of accessibility and the absence of people with disabilities. Sayable claims about inaccessibility solidify people with disabilities into a category that is justified as "essentially excludable." Writing programs should not participate in the justification of exclusion but rather serve as leaders in noticing the absence of accessibility and students with disabilities in our buildings, classrooms, curricula, technologies, and values. By challenging justifications of exclusion, "perhaps we can begin to remake that which has conditioned consciousness by telling a new story about who and where we are" (91).

Bureaucracies structure students with disabilities as not only partial participants in space but also in time. In Titchkosky's interpretive scenes, access is repeatedly postponed. In exploring this concept, she recounts her experience of advocating for notifications of closures of accessible washrooms. If students who rely on accessible washrooms are not notified of their closures, they cannot participate. When bringing this matter to the attention of the university, she heard a variety of arguments that rely on the contraction and expansion of all—"should 'all' students receive notifications of accessible washroom closures when they already receive too many emails?" and "We are not just talking about access to washrooms here; we need to talk about 'all' matters of exclusion" (106). While all gets contracted and expanded to determine an appropriate bureaucratic measure, the students who depend upon accessible washrooms disappear. Titchkosky argues that perceiving access in relation to "all" reveals that "disability, unlike window cleaning, is not yet imagined as an essential aspect of all of our lives" (109). In another interpretive scene, students who brought movable desks into the hallway outside a flexible classroom agree to move their desks for the students who use wheelchairs and canes, but only when they arrive. Through the lens of "When?" we see access as a contingency, as something that needs to be dealt with "not yet" but when those students arrive. While arguments for universal design and flexibility are useful for making accessibility relevant to all, Titchkosky warns that these arguments can postpone access, and in the meantime, individuals who really need it disappear.

Conceptualizing access as interpretive relations between bodies and spaces should not sound unfamiliar to professionals in our field. We have long been attuned to the socially situated nature of learning and identity, and we are always negotiating our values within bureaucratic spaces. Yet writing programs themselves can function as bureaucracies that treat disability as an individual problem to be fixed. Rather than reinforcing a bureaucratic approach to disability that solely relies on accommodating individual problems, we need to employ a conceptual framework for access as an act of perception at all levels of writing programs, from how we design our curriculum to our teacher preparation and models for instruction. When instructors say, "But I wasn't prepared to work with students with disabilities," we hear a cry for information about individual disabilities and strategies. We need to refocus instructors' attention away from accommodating individuals toward the spaces, times, and social environments we construct in our programs, buildings, and classrooms that create disability and inaccessibility.

Rather than ignoring or dismissing bureaucratic and individualized approaches to disability, we need to engage them as part of the current perceptual landscape of access. Individual accommodations are useful for many students, but our work does not stop there. We must turn the attention of our leaders and instructors to locating disability and inaccessibility in our collective interrelatedness because as Titchkosky says, "It is in culture, in the midst of others, that disability is made; in this way, we are never alone in our bodies" (59).

Works Cited

Madden, Shannon, and Wood, Tara. "Suggested Practices for Syllabus Accessibility Statements." *Kairos: Rhetoric, Technology, and Pedagogy PraxisWiki*, vol. 18, no. 1, Fall 2013.

Wood, Tara, Dolmage, Jay, Price, Margaret, & Lewiecki-Wilson, Cynthia. "Where We Are: Disability and Accessibility." *Composition Studies*, vol. 42, no. 2, 2014, pp. 147–50.

Annika Konrad is a PhD candidate in Composition and Rhetoric at University of Wisconsin–Madison. Her writing on the rhetorical experiences of people who are blind and visually impaired has appeared in Reflections *and will be reprinted in* Best of the Journals in Rhetoric and Composition *(Parlor Press).*

Review

Centering Madness in the Academe: Supporting and Learning from Mental Disability

Elisabeth L. Miller

Price, Margaret. *Mad at School: Rhetorics of Mental Disability and Academic Life*. University of Michigan Press, 2011. 271 pages.

Universities are known as institutions of the mind. Teacher-scholars make a living by using their minds. Students, at least in the context of a liberal education, attend universities to expand their minds. So what does it mean, in the spaces of academe, to have a disability that affects one's mind? Margaret Price asks this important question in *Mad at School: Rhetorics of Mental Disability and Academic Life*. In answering that question, Price exposes ableist "norms" at the core of academic discourse and higher education in general. Assumptions about energy and collegiality permeate our job postings, requirements for interviews and campus visits, and hiring decisions. Our environmental expectations demand comfortable-looking social performances at conferences and speedy production of scholarship. In our classrooms, we assess students for reasoned ways of speaking up and adherence to attendance requirements. In the most extreme of contexts mental illness lurks behind conversations about campus violence.

These assumptions and exclusions must concern writing program administrators as we support teachers, conceive of curricula that impacts students across the university, and manage the substantial demands of our work. *Mad at School* is an important resource for enabling us to both include and learn from individuals with mental disabilities. Price's primary contribution is a sharp critique of the ableism undergirding many of the most basic assumptions of higher education, and an insistence that educators not only critique, but do something about these inequities (57). Price accomplishes this scholarly, pedagogical, and activist work in an introduction, six robust chapters, and a succinct conclusion pointing to further avenues for research and teaching. Each chapter focuses on varied sites, forwarding "not a single sustained argument," but a "kind of smorgasbord" (21) of issues, needs, and implications for mental disability in higher education. Price uses critical discourse analysis (CDA) as her method and methodology, analyzing "rich features and salient patterns" of texts (Barton 23). That practice leads her to pinpoint several common topoi of academic discourse that mental disability challenges: "rationality, criticality, presence, participation, productivity, collegiality, security, coherence, truth, and independence" (30).

From the important critical work of *Mad at School*, I highlight three primary moves instructive for the theory and practice of writing program administration: 1) challenging norms of academic discourse; 2) offering suggestions for improving access in the everyday spaces of higher education for students and academic professionals with mental disabilities; and 3) turning beyond the everyday to spaces of crisis, self-representation, and independence and exclusion to learn from mental disability.

Price first employs CDA to interrogate how academic discourse conflicts with mental disability. In her first chapter, "Listening to the Subject of Mental Disability," Price joins conversations in disability rhetoric initiated by Catherine Prendergast and Cynthia Lewiecki-Wilson to assert that mental disability affects individuals' "rhetoricity"—or their ability to be perceived as capable of producing rhetoric, to be listened to. She then explores how various discourses perpetuate that loss of rhetoricity. Psychiatric discourse (such as the Diagnostic and Statistical Manual of Mental Disabilities, or DSM) as well as approaches taken up in rhetoric and composition, including Berlin's "rhetoric of reason" and various tenets of critical pedagogy, assume reasoned discourse and rational subjects as a starting point, excluding "the mad subject in academic discourse" (37). Likewise, Price argues that pedagogies of listening (Lee, Ratcliffe), while they decenter rationality, still fail to address a central question of rhetoricity and mental disability: "What happens to the rhetor who *cannot* be 'listened' to—because ze is not present, or fails to participate in discussions, or fails to 'make sense' on a neurotypical scale?" (44).

After challenging the very foundations of academic discourse, Price turns to the practical heart of *Mad at School* in chapters 2 and 3: a critique of the inaccessibility of academic spaces for students and teacher-scholar-administrators with mental disabilities. Here she provides myriad strategies for "ways to move" toward more equitable access. The difficulty of ensuring access in academic spaces is made vivid through Price's conception of "kairotic spaces": the "less formal, often unnoticed, areas of academe where knowledge is produced and power is exchanged" (60). These environments and situations (e.g., classroom discussions, office hours, academic conferences, and job interviews) are unscripted, but they have serious consequences for students' grades and identities, and for scholars' professional advancement. Kairotic spaces are about timing, combining an expectation for *"spontaneity with high levels of professional/academic impact"* (61; emphasis original).

For students, kairotic spaces rely on the topoi of presence and participation, each grounded in a number of ableist expectations—particularly for attendance and classroom discussion. Presence is taken "as an a priori good" (64). Students who fail to be present are perceived to be unmotivated, underachieving, or simply bad (65). While Price does not argue that we should remove all attendance requirements, she urges educators to critique the logics underlying our insistence on presence as a physical performance and as the baseline for student success. Price also challenges educators to rethink participation (beyond the sharing of ideas verbally through rational discussion). What appears disruptive to our standards of normal academic participation *"might in fact be a student participating* in a way that performs, or attempts to accommodate, her own mental disability" (74; emphasis original). What educators interpret as rude whispering or note-passing "may be efforts to 'catch up' on discussion that is progressing too fast to follow; they might also signal that a student cannot speak in front of the group but deeply wishes to express some idea" (74). Even cell phone use may actually help a student stay active in thought or work through classroom anxiety.

For teachers or administrators wondering how to rethink classroom topoi such as presence and participation, a 15-page section of *Mad at School*, "A Way to Move: Redesigning the Kairotic Space of the Classroom," is an invaluable resource. Drawing on universal design (See Dolmage; Womack; Blevins), Price offers multiple suggestions to create environments that are "accessible to all learning styles, abilities, and personalities" (87). These ideas offer not a fail-safe checklist to reach inclusion, but rather ways to engage in the "consistent effort" of creating access for students (and oneself as the teacher) (87). (See also Annika Konrad.)

Among myriad compelling ideas, Price argues for demystifying the kairotic spaces of your classroom. What are your norms for class discussion? How will class material be shared – online, in handouts, in discussion? Explain what participation and presence means in your classroom, and provide various channels for both. For instance, consider offering the option for online discussion even during in-person class sessions. Price's own requirements for participation include assigning annotation of documents to engage students as "active interveners in texts" with details for these annotations helpfully included in Appendix A and B (93). Participation can be made increasingly accessible by having students call upon one another, asking for volunteer note-takers for discussions, or using response cards on which students hold up answers or write notes to the instructor. Opening multiple channels of communication—offering online chat office hours, for one—may also mitigate anxiety and improve communication for students and instructors. Most importantly, teachers must understand that not all instructional and communicative approaches work for all students (or all instructors). Teachers "committed to creating more accessible kairotic spaces for those with mental disabilities" are not "'solving problems,'" but rather "finding ways to move" (101).

Access in academe also matters for scholar-teacher-administrators with mental disabilities. In chapter 3, "The Essential Functions of the Position," Price interrogates the meaning and implications of the Americans with Disabilities Act's requirement that individuals be able to perform "the essential functions of the job." She questions how our understanding of essential functions conflicts with and excludes mental disability. The academic job search and participation in academic conferences are two particularly exclusionary cases. Both are kairotic spaces, requiring performances of collegiality and productivity that are judged with real consequences: being hired or tenured (or not). Learning from mental disability, Price offers a range of "recommendations for professional practice" (129), including an increased focus on listening—at interpersonal and structural levels. In addition to rethinking time and other constraints on tenure, Price suggests focusing mentoring relationships on accessibility—"responsive to ways of learning, social styles, and communication preferences" (139). In essence, writing program administrators must not limit a focus on universal design to the classroom but extend that commitment to all of their work with students and teachers.

The everyday spaces of academe challenge educators to rethink assumptions about mental disability, rationality, and more. So, too, do our ongoing discussions around crisis and violence in higher education. Chapter 4, "Assaults on the Ivory Tower," addresses mass school shootings at Virginia Tech and Northern Illinois University. Analyzing media portrayals of the student shooters in both cases, Price explores how "madness is generally assumed to be the *cause* of the shooters' actions," relegating mental disability to "a space of unrecoverable deviance" (144–45; emphasis original). Price persuasively demonstrates how linking mental disability, violence, and campus safety infringes upon students' privacy—their diagnoses, writing, and more. Specifically, the practice of treating students' writing as symptoms and prioritizing the referring of potentially mad or ill students to medical resources further divides students with mental disabilities from the norms of academe. While providing students with access to resources is undoubtedly an important part of our role as teachers, Price argues that viewing individuals with mental disability as sources of violence fails to address "[l]arger social forces contributing to a culture of violence" (175).

In her two closing chapters, Price represents the voices and experiences of people with mental disabilities—particularly outside of academe. Chapter 5, "Her Pronouns Wax and Wane," examines three autobiographies composed by women with mental disabilities. Price analyzes how the authors inventively employ shifts between pronouns to assert their own counter-diagnosis, challenging topoi of coherence and truth. This chapter contributes to work on disability memoir and offers a potential essay for students to read as a model of close rhetorical analysis. Price moves into a qualitative study in Chapter 6, "In/ter/dependent Scholarship." Focusing on the experiences of three independent scholars with mental disabilities, Price employs accessible methodology—co-determining with participants the modes for interviews and co-analyzing the data. Collaboratively, Price and these three independent scholars examine topoi of independence in academe and how norms around scholarship, publication, productivity, and credentials often bar individuals with mental disabilities from participation. Conversely, the role of independent scholar offers a critique of those academic norms and an important venue for scholarship outside of the constraints of higher education.

The scope of *Mad at School* is at once admirably broad and pragmatically specific: critiquing the adherence to rationality and norms in academic discourse and providing ways to move toward access for students and teachers. What's more, Price's passion for bringing mental disability to the forefront of our discussions about higher education is apparent. "I wrote this book because I could not go any longer without writing it," says Price in the last line of her introduction (24). She similarly explains a deep commitment to including her final chapter focused on the experiences of independent scholars with mental disabilities "because, quite simply, I could not bear to publish this book without careful attention to those who operate outside the privileged borders of academe" (22). Careful attention is indeed what *Mad at School* offers: attention to people with mental disabilities, the challenges they face in higher education discourses and spaces, and the significant insight that they have to offer to educators and administrators—particularly in Writing Studies. Price urges each of us to pay attention, take action, and learn, reminding us that both listening and trying are necessary to support our diverse bodies and minds in the university: "we must try, think, query, flex, observe, listen, and try again" (101). That is the effort and ethical commitment that access requires and that we all—our students, ourselves, and our colleagues—deserve.

Works Cited

Barton, Ellen. "Inductive Discourse Analysis: Discovering Rich Features." *Discourse Studies in Composition*, edited by Ellen Barton and Gail Stygall. Hampton Press, 2002, pp. 19–42.

Berlin, James. "Contemporary Composition: The Major Pedagogical Theories." *College English*, vol. 44, no. 8, 1982, pp. 765–77.

Dolmage, Jay. "Disability Studies Pedagogy, Usability and Universal Design." *Disability Studies Quarterly*, vol. 25, no. 4, 2005, dsq-sds.org/article/view/627/804.

Lee, Amy. *Composing Critical Pedagogies: Teaching Writing as Revision*. NCTE, 2000.

Lewiecki-Wilson, Cynthia. "Rethinking Rhetoric through Mental Disabilities." *Rhetoric Review*, vol. 22, no. 2, 2003, pp. 154–202.

Prendergast, Catherine. "On the Rhetorics of Mental Disability." *Embodied Rhetorics: Disability in Language and Culture*, edited by James Wilson and Cynthia Lewiecki-Wilson, SIUP, 2001, pp. 45–60.

Ratcliffe, Krista. *Rhetorical Listening: Identification, Gender, Whiteness*. SIUP, 2005.

Womack, Anne-Marie. "Teaching Is Accommodation: Universally Designing Composition Classrooms and Syllabi." *College Composition and Communication*. vol. 68, no. 3, 2017, pp. 494–525.

Elisabeth Miller is an Assistant Professor of English at University of Nevada, Reno, a land-grant, public, research university. She researches and teaches about literacy, disability, and community engagement. Her work has appeared in College English, Community Literacy Journal, *and* Writing Lab Newsletter.

Review

Making Space to Engage Difference in the Classroom

Kelly A. Whitney

Kerschbaum, Stephanie L. *Toward a New Rhetoric of Difference*. NCTE, 2014. 185 pages.

Stephanie L. Kerschbaum's *Toward a New Rhetoric of Difference* comes at an important moment as composition studies grapples with ways to make first-year composition, and broader frameworks for postsecondary education, more inclusive. This movement toward inclusion has manifested in revised syllabi and reading lists that make space for a variety of perspectives and knowledges from traditionally marginalized populations, disciplinary statements that endorse students' various languages ("Students' Rights"), and assignments that interrogate relationships between language, power, and knowledge. While these efforts have been crucial to the field's commitment to diversity, scholars continue to call for more comprehensive approaches to course design that build difference into the curriculum itself (see Brueggeman and Lewiecki-Wilson; Coombs; Inoue; Price). Kerschbaum offers composition's disciplinary and pedagogic commitments to difference a critical and crucial examination of what it means—and what it takes—to weave difference into the fabric of pedagogic practice. This book challenges composition instructors and scholars and writing program administrators to adopt an orientation toward difference that enables a classroom culture founded on what she calls an "ethic of answerable engagement." Consequently, this book marks an important shift in how we as a field recognize, narrate, and value difference.

Readers who are familiar with Kerschbaum's work will recognize her definition of difference as *dynamic, relational, and emergent*, a definition that departs from traditional conceptions of difference as *static* or *self-evident* (56; see also Kerschbaum, "Avoiding"). Difference is always in-the-making, she argues, and it is through interaction that differences come to matter. To illustrate how differences are emergent rather than fixed, she offers a personal anecdote wherein she details some of the ways she identifies (deaf, White, female, glasses-wearer, Midwesterner) and claims these features come to matter interactionally. She explains:

> As I move in and out of different situations, some of them matter more at some times and less at others, and they take on different shades of meaning and nuance depending on who I am interacting with. That I wear glasses is inconsequential in most interactions, whereas the fact that I'm deaf matters significantly more often. But how these things matter is highly variable. (65)

Because certain features come to matter differently in different situations and interactions, she turns her readers' attention not necessarily to what makes a feature different but, more importantly, how a feature emerges as different. Extending this concept of difference as dynamic, relational, and emergent to the classroom, therefore, opens up possibilities for exploring how differences come to matter in students' interactions. As students recognize the "rhetorical cues that signal the presence of difference," they respond to these cues by asserting themselves in ways they want others to notice (57).

Kerschbaum recognizes that institutional discourses on diversity assume difference not as dynamic, relational, and emergent but as "something owned by individuals who have particular differences" (36). Through a textual analysis of her institution's diversity agenda statement, she finds that institutional diversity discourses, which reveal globalization and neoliberal influences and commitments (see also Gallagher; Slaughter and Rhoades), claim to value diversity because of what diversity adds to the university experience for students. As universities take action to improve diversity, real, lived experiences and bodies become reduced to categories of race and ethnicity, reminiscent of "add [race, ethnicity, gender] and stir" approaches to incorporating difference. While this method certainly improves the number of traditionally underrepresented bodies on campus, it functions as an institutional accommodation to difference rather than making an accommodating institution (see also Price). Kerschbaum's analysis of her institution's diversity agenda serves as an excellent model for how WPAs might analyze their own local institutional discourses that influence their programs and classrooms, and, more importantly, her analysis identifies the limitations of institutional diversity commitments that commodify diverse bodies as "stable, objectively real things that persist across time, rather than as historically and locally situated human creations" (39). Institutional discourses on diversity, therefore, fail to engage difference on a structural or institutional level in any meaningful way yet, she claims, they continue to influence how others understand and experience diversity.

While she recognizes the limitations of institutional discourses that mark difference through race and ethnicity, she is careful not to dismiss category identifications; rather, she claims that category identifications allow us to "acknowledg[e] the way categories help us negotiate situations while holding those category identifications open for new interpretation and understanding" (92). That is, when difference is understood as dynamic, emergent, and relational, we shift our attention to how these markers of difference come to matter in a particular interaction. Rather than eliding difference or simply acknowledging difference exists, an ethic of answerable engagement calls on students and teachers "to identify how they are naming, conveying, describing, and articulating difference in everyday interaction" (78). Markers of difference, therefore, become the starting point of engagement as we pay attention to how these markers come to matter and how we position ourselves through the interaction.

To develop her concept of difference, Kerschbaum examines students' interactions and how they recognize and respond to emerging differences during peer review sessions in a first-year composition course. As a frequent research site since the process movement, peer review has contributed significant insight into how students engage with their own and other's writing, and Kerschbaum contributes to this larger conversation "a complex dynamic in which relationships and positions, the very material of identity formation, emerged during interaction" (18). For example, in one of several interactions she analyzes, Kerschbaum discusses how two students, Blia and Choua, read each other's differences and position themselves within their interaction as they debate the placement of a comma. This interaction, Kerschbaum claims, "addresses not just whether a comma should appear, but also who gets to claim authority regarding the comma use" (94–5). The manner in which these students talk over the other, use first-person plural or first-person singular, and invoke proper grammar rules or previous writing instruction all speak back to "how students mark their own and others' differences to marshal authority in the midst of disagreement" (98). In other words, through each exchange in an interaction, students come to recognize differences, and in light of how they interpret these differences, (re)position themselves as the authoritative figure in the exchange.

While this moment of disagreement could serve as an opportunity for students to explore how they are marking each other's differences and how they are positioning themselves in response to these emerging differences, Kerschbaum finds that none of the exchanges she observed led to meaningful engagements with difference. This finding speaks back to what many composition instructors may recognize as students' often contradicting views on difference. While many Millennial students claim to value differences, they also often claim, perhaps in an effort to appear colorblind, that differences don't matter (Pew). These contradicting views make engaging with difference in the classroom particularly challenging. In this study, for example, students decide to move on to another topic instead of engaging their disagreements. In the end, disagreements "did not seem likely to lead to long-lasting change in perspective or orientation to a text" (98). Adopting an ethic of answerable engagement, however, can bring into relief these contradicting views on difference by promoting individual responsibility to account for how differences come to matter without presupposing differences as always already existing.

Analyzing students' interactions during peer review allows Kerschbaum to tacitly remind her readers that opportunities to engage with difference are already prevalent in our classrooms and that adopting her conception of difference doesn't require a revised curriculum. Instead, recognizing these rhetorical performances—or how students position themselves as differences come to matter—requires us to shift what we hear in the classroom and how we hear it. To adopt an ethic of answerable engagement, then, requires what she calls "flexible listening," an approach to learning with students that pushes back on prescriptive ways of knowing about students. Echoing Ratcliffe's rhetorical listening, flexible listening challenges us to reconcile that what we have come to recognize and know about students rests on experiential, disciplinary, and institutional narratives *about* students (see also Price). To open up what we listen to requires us to shift from "learning about" students to "learning with" them, which also leads us to ask questions such as "How are individuals positioned by others?" instead of "What groups do individuals belong to?" (74)

By focusing on the how instead of the what, Kerschbaum invites reflection and consideration on the ways we articulate what we as composition instructors, scholars, and administrators do and value. For example, explaining to students that the goal of peer review is to improve a peer's writing has effects on how students approach this particular activity. This articulation opens up possibilities for engagement—namely, for students to figure out ways to make the paper better—but also closes off other possibilities for engagement. To promote an ethic of answerable engagement, she claims, requires significant reflection on and accountability for how we narrate our work and our students to each other. Therefore, while what we do in the classroom might not necessarily change, how we articulate what we do shapes the classroom discourses and how students structure their interactions.

Toward a New Rhetoric of Difference is a pivotal text that will shift the standards on disciplinary and pedagogic engagements with difference. For WPAs, this book invites critical programmatic reflection and serves as a cautionary tale for how institutional discourses on diversity structure others' orientations toward difference. For composition instructors both seasoned and novice, it illustrates the robust opportunities to engage difference in our classrooms. For scholars, it's a crucial reminder that how we narrate students in our scholarship has effects on what we as a field do and value. This book is required reading for those who are committed to pushing back on neoliberal logics of difference and embracing ethical and responsible engagements of difference.

WORKS CITED

Brueggeman, Branda, and Cindy Lewiecki-Wilson, editors. *Disability and the Teaching of Writing: A Critical Sourcebook.* Beford St. Martin's, 2006.

Conference on College Composition and Communication. "Students' Right to Their Own Language." *College Composition and Communication*, vol. 25, no. 3, 1974, pp. 1–32.

Coombs, Norman. *Making Online Teaching Accessible: Inclusive Course Design for Students with Disabilities.* Jossey-Bass, 2010.

Gallagher, Chris W. "Being There: (Re)Making the Assessment Scene." *College Composition and Communication*, vol. 63, no. 3, 2011, pp. 450–76.

Inoue, Asao B. *Antiracist Writing Assessment Ecologies: Teaching and Assessing Writing for a Socially Just Future.* Parlor P, 2015.

Kerschbaum, Stephanie L. "Avoiding the Difference Fixation: Identity Categories, Markers of Difference, and the Teaching of Writing." *College Composition and Communication*, vol. 63, no. 4, 2012, pp. 616–44.

Pew Research Center. "On Views of Race and Inequality, Blacks and Whites are Worlds Apart." Pew Research Center's Social & Demographic Trends Project. 27 June 2016, pewrsr.ch/28XRKLq. Accessed 28 February 2017.

Price, Margaret. *Mad at School: Rhetorics of Mental Disability and Academic Life.* U of Michigan P, 2011.

Ratcliffe, Krista. *Rhetorical Listening: Identification, Gender, Whiteness.* SIUP, 2005.

Slaughter, Sheila, and Gary Rhoades. *Academic Capitalism and the New Economy.* Johns Hopkins UP, 2004.

Kelly A. Whitney is a doctoral candidate in Rhetoric and Professional Communication at New Mexico State University, a comprehensive, land-grant, research university. Her research centers on ontology and epistemology in scientific and medical discourses, particularly as studied through feminist and disability rhetorics. Her current research examines the rhetorical-material emergence, function, and circulation of women's preventive health practices.

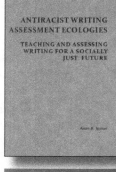

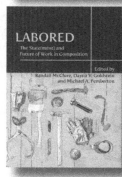
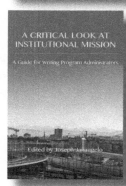